MANCHESTER CITY
OUR DECADE

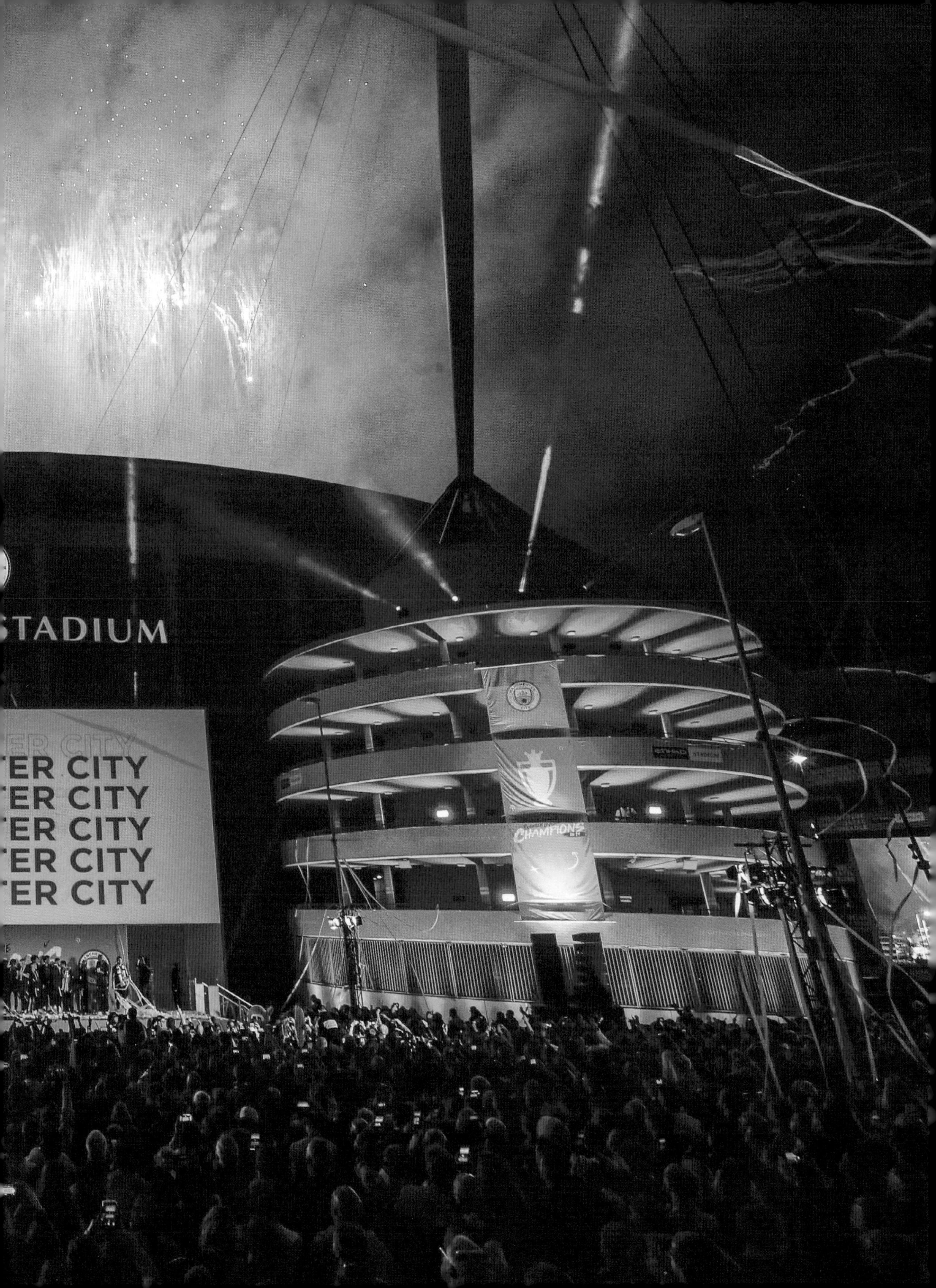
STADIUM
ER CITY
ER CITY
ER CITY
ER CITY
ER CITY
CHAMPIONS

MANCHESTER CITY
OUR DECADE
A JOURNEY TO THE SUMMIT OF ENGLISH FOOTBALL

BY
ROB POLLARD

Reach Sport

MANCHESTER CITY
OUR DECADE
A JOURNEY TO THE SUMMIT OF ENGLISH FOOTBALL

Writer: Rob Pollard
Photography: Victoria Haydn, Tom Flathers, Matt McNulty and Sharon Lathom
Additional imagery with thanks to Getty Images and PA Images
Production Editor: Nick Moreton
Additional production: Roy Gilfoyle
Design: Colin Harrison
Cover Design: Amit Patel

First published in Great Britain and Ireland in 2022
by Reach Sport, a part of Reach PLC Ltd

www.reachsport.com

Hardback ISBN: 9781914197222
Printed by Bell & Bain

FOREWORDS

HEROES AND OUR DECADE MOMENTS

CONTENTS

BY

Khaldoon Al Mubarak

I **feel extremely proud and privileged to be able to write the foreword to this celebration of Manchester City's successes over the last decade.**

The winning of the FA Cup in 2011 was a watershed moment – It was our first trophy in 35 years. The ten years that followed, saw Manchester City go on to become the dominant side in English football. This book is therefore a celebration of the collective efforts and achievement of so many during that period. My hope is that it serves as a reminder to us all of the incredible journey that we have shared.

Winning the Premier League in 2012 with 'that goal' saw us end our 44-year wait for a league title and was the first real indication that Manchester City was an organisation now capable of performing consistently at the highest level. It was therefore also a sign that our Club was well positioned to secure even more silverware and to start to achieve the vision that His Highness Sheikh Mansour had set in 2008.

Since that win over QPR, in what was perhaps the most iconic day in Premier League history, we've won another four Premier League titles, one FA Cup, six League Cups, three Community Shields and reached our first ever Champions League final. It is a remarkable set of achievements and unrivalled in English football over the decade.

We've come a long way in a relatively short space of time, and I am so honoured to have been part of it. The hard work and successes of Roberto Mancini, Manuel Pellegrini and now Pep Guardiola mean that our club is in a wonderful position to continue growing, developing and, of course, winning. I want to thank all three of them for their dedication and hard work.

On behalf of His Highness Sheikh Mansour, I also want to take this opportunity to express sincere thanks and appreciation to the Board, and every executive and employee for playing their part in the achievements of the last ten years. Each trophy is testament to, and a product of, the work of everyone within our City family - all striving to deliver on a shared vision of success for our Club.

Importantly we have tried always to remain true to our values and it is this context that makes our steady and consistent achievements all the more pleasing. Our commitment to those values will remain undiminished as will our ongoing commitment to innovation and constantly challenging ourselves to be better and to do better – both on the field and off it.

Thank you for your support throughout the last 10 years. Every achievement is because of you and for you.

Here's to the decades that lie ahead.

Khaldoon Al Mubarak

BY

Rob Pollard

t's been a pleasure and privilege to be a Manchester City fan throughout my life, but never more so than during the last decade, a golden period which has seen us establish ourselves as the pre-eminent side in English football.

No one should forget the darker days. Our spiral down the divisions, the multiple managerial failures and near daily disasters. They make today's success taste all the sweeter.

But the last decade has been remarkable, by anyone's standards. Who else can say they won the league for the first time in 44 years in the final seconds of the season, pipping their greatest rivals in the process, or indeed collected 198 points over the course of two successive Premier League campaigns, providing a new measure of what is required to be champions of England? Whether it's drama or greatness you're after, City have delivered spectacularly.

This book's focus is on the last 10 seasons (all the statistics and information are correct up to and including May 29 2021), but the story would not be complete without a look at three vital matches towards the end of the 2010-11 season: our FA Cup semi-final and final victories that ended 35 years without a trophy, and the narrow win over Tottenham that ensured we qualified for the Champions League for the first time in its current guise.

Those matches laid the platform for the decade of success that followed...*Our Decade*.

We've had three managers during the period under discussion here and each of them has played a significant role.

Roberto Mancini had arguably the hardest task. The Italian had to root out an inferiority complex and transform a club known for abject failure into winners. He did it and did so in memorable fashion. Every manager who follows Roberto now has an easier job thanks to the firm foundations he laid.

Our first trophy in 35 years was delivered in the form of the 2011 FA Cup, and twelve months later our first league trophy in 44 years arrived in special circumstances. They were heady days, with the majority of our fanbase taking a step into the

trophy-winning unknown. It felt exciting and new, and it was all fronted by a manager who was sophisticated and stylish.

His successor Manuel Pellegrini then accelerated our move towards a more attacking game. The handbrake came off under the Chilean's watch, and his first season – criminally underrated in my opinion – was incredibly enjoyable.

He became the first City manager since Joe Mercer in 1970 to deliver two trophies in a single season as we scored 157 goals in all competitions in 2013-14.

And what is left to say about Pep Guardiola? The greatest manager in the world at present – possibly of all time – and the man who has revolutionised our football club. We haven't just won consistently under the Catalan's leadership, we have done so with remarkable style.

The Centurions campaign of 2017-18 saw City rewrite the history books, setting a series of new Premier League records – most points, goals and wins – and we followed that up by becoming the first team in English football history to secure all four domestic trophies in a single season. Over the course of those two years, we collected 198 points. No side in the history of English football can match that consistency and the bar was raised in terms of what is needed to be champions.

And Guardiola continues to strive for more. He signed a new deal in November 2020 and his five full seasons at Manchester City are already the most he's spent at any club since becoming a manager. It's fair to say he has changed the very fabric of our football club and we will reap the rewards of his management for many years after he departs.

Writing this book has been a pleasure. As much as you think you remember everything about such a wonderful period in our storied history, there are always moments that evade you. Raking over the past has never felt so good.

There are a number of people without whom writing this book would not have been possible and I would like to extend my

thanks to each and every one of them.

I sought the opinion of a number of City fans before embarking on the project. They were, in no particular order, Liam Wright, Andrew Green, Jonathan Derbyshire, Daniel Mallard, Mike Hammond, Andy MacNab and Murdoch Dalziel. They helped me curate the list of Our Heroes and Our Days that make up the essence of the book, and so it felt right to get them to contribute their memories and experiences of that wonderful period we have all enjoyed so much. I have weaved in their recollections where appropriate and I'm sure everyone would agree they have added something special.

Neil Leigh's subediting skills were essential. Thank you so much, Neil, for your contribution. Chris Bailey is a friend and mentor, without whom I would not have been able to take this project on, and Toby Craig's help was vital and hugely appreciated. And thank you to Victoria Haydn, Sharon Lathom, Tom Flathers and Matt McNulty – the best photography team in the Premier League – for the wonderful imagery.

A big thank you as well to Alex and the team at Wine & Wallop in Didsbury – they have offered me endless coffee, electricity and warmth. I've written more of this book in there than anywhere else. For some reason, I found myself at my most productive when inside that fine pub!

And finally, thank you to my family and friends for their patience. In particular, my mum, dad, sister Jade, Ed, Jonny and Dhivya have been incredibly encouraging and helpful. This project has been a real labour of love, but they supported me throughout.

I hope you enjoy *Our Decade*. Whether you learn something new or simply indulge in beautiful nostalgia, I sincerely want this book to remind City fans across the world of the drama and greatness we have witnessed together. It's been one hell of a ride.

Rob Pollard

MICAH RICHARDS

Has there been a more beloved academy graduate in City's recent history than Micah Richards? With his wide smile and infectious laugh, happiness follows the former City central-defender wherever he goes.

Richards, raised in Leeds, joined City as a 14-year-old. Spotted playing for Oldham, he elected to join City's academy setup because of our reputation for nurturing raw talent. He stood out among his peers thanks to his athleticism and physique and went on to make his first-team debut at Highbury as a substitute during a 1-0 defeat to Arsenal in October 2005.

His debut for England Under-21s came against Moldova in August 2006, and a full England cap followed in a 1-1 draw with Holland not long after, when at just 18 years old, he became the youngest defender to ever represent the Three Lions.

Fast-forward to 2008 and the question each existing player was asking in light of the club's takeover by the Abu Dhabi United Group was: am I capable of keeping my place now City's squad is being revamped?

Richards' answer was emphatic. While others fell away, unable to compete with the new talent coming into the club, he went from strength to strength. By the time Roberto Mancini joined in late 2009 and the revolution really gathered pace, he was one of England's top defenders.

He was central to both our 2011 FA Cup success and the unforgettable 2012 Premier League title win.

His best game was perhaps the marauding performance at Old Trafford in 2011-12 when City won 6-1 and sent an unmistakable message to the established elite in England that we were title contenders. It was the day the balance of power in Manchester shifted and Richards

> "City has always been my spiritual home and where I enjoyed my best years as a player"

was unplayable, with his relentless forays down the right causing United significant damage.

Ultimately, however, a series of injuries – and the form of Pablo Zabaleta – meant he was no longer first choice at right-back. He was subsequently loaned to Fiorentina in Italy's Serie A for the entirety of the 2014-15 season, before being sold to Aston Villa, where he spent three years battling a knee problem.

"City has always been my spiritual home and where I enjoyed my best years as a player," Richards said when announcing his retirement from the game in July 2019. "Being part of the side that ended the long wait for silverware – in 2011 and 2012 – was very special. It kick-started this new era and the club has never looked back. What has happened since has been amazing."

After more than 240 appearances for City and 13 for England, Richards is now one of the game's leading pundits. He was barely off both UK and US screens during the 2020-21 season – and his likeability and insight means that's unlikely to change any time soon.

After his rapid early rise, Richards' career was cruelly impacted by injury, but his legacy at City remains strong. An academy graduate who improved our side drastically under Stuart Pearce and Sven-Goran Eriksson, he was one of the few who managed to make the grade at City post-takeover.

His contribution to our success was clear.

JOE HART

Joe Hart returned from a loan spell at Birmingham at the start of the 2010-11 season and was installed as City's No.1, replacing Shay Given.

"Mancini saw something in me, and I'll be forever grateful," Hart says. "I thought my City career had ended but he said, 'I want to bring you back for pre-season and look at you more closely'."

His first game saw him produce an outstanding display as we drew 0-0 at Tottenham, making a string of saves that defied belief. It was a sign of things to come. From then on, he was central to our success for the next six years, helping City to two Premier League titles, an FA Cup and a League Cup, as well as winning the Premier League Golden Glove award on four occasions.

> "If I could do the celebrations again I would. I didn't know what to do, I was dumbfounded. When you've worked so hard for something and it comes off, you don't know what to do"

Our 2011 FA Cup win owed much to his ability. He kept five clean sheets in eight matches, including in the semi-final victory over Manchester United and the final against Stoke.

"Winning the FA Cup was hard to take in," he says. "If I could do the celebrations again I would. I didn't know what to do, I was dumbfounded. When you've worked so hard for something and it comes off, you don't know what to do."

He played every Premier League game the following season as we won the title in dramatic fashion. His joyous celebratory sprint around the Etihad after Sergio Aguero's 93.20 winner remains iconic – and perfectly encapsulated the euphoric mood of all City fans that unforgettable afternoon.

But there are two performances which stand out and will live long in the memory of all City fans, both of which saw Hart produce an almost superhuman display.

The first came against Borussia Dortmund in 2012. The German side completely outplayed City, only to be thwarted time and again by an inspired Hart. The match, somehow, finished 1-1, with Mario Balotelli's late penalty preserving our 17-game unbeaten run at home in Europe.

The second came at the Camp Nou, as Hart and Lionel Messi engaged in a personal duel. His performance there, in one of the most iconic arenas in world football, was virtuoso.

The arrival of Pep Guardiola in 2016 saw Hart's time as City's undisputed first-choice 'keeper come to an end. The new manager wanted a sweeper-keeper, one comfortable in possession. That wasn't Hart's game, and after loan spells at Torino and West Ham, he joined Burnley in 2018.

"I've always loved the Manchester City fans," he says. "I came as a kid from Shrewsbury Town and it was the pinnacle for me to be at this club and that was before challenging for titles. I was welcomed from day one and the fans saw me as someone who would try his best. I couldn't have done the things I've done if I hadn't been embraced."

Having joined City as a raw teenager in the summer of 2006, over the course of 12 magical years at the Etihad, Hart cemented his status as another true City icon and a goalkeeper of the very highest calibre.

VINCENT KOMPANY

"I don't feel English but I definitely feel Manc," Vincent Kompany said when launching his testimonial match in 2019, an event that saw 51,602 pack into the Etihad Stadium to celebrate his 11-year association with City, the proceeds of which went to Tackle4MCR, the charity he set up in conjunction with the city's mayor, Andy Burnham.

It was typical of Kompany. His popularity across the city – not just with City fans – meant the game would always prove to be a big draw, and he used the opportunity to support a local cause, underlining his selflessness and love of Manchester.

He married Carla Higgs, Manchester born and bred and lifelong City supporter, and immersed himself in the city's culture from day one. In 2018, he graduated from Manchester Business School with an MBA. Coming to the Etihad wasn't just a career move, it was a new life for a man whose leadership and defensive qualities were the bedrock on which so much of our success was built.

Kompany joined from Hamburg in 2008, days before the takeover the club was completed. He played initially in midfield, but Roberto Mancini moved him to centre-half when he became City manager in late 2009. It proved a masterstroke.

His defining qualities were his grit, determination, ability to defend, leadership and quality on the ball. He would drag us through matches at times, with his desire and will to win unparalleled.

But his propensity for scoring vital goals deepened the bond between player and supporters. His header in the 1-0 victory at home to Manchester United moved us tantalisingly close to the title in 2012, the winner in by far our most difficult remaining obstacle. He also scored on the day

"He defines the essence of the club. For a decade he has been the lifeblood"

we clinched the 2014 title at home to West Ham and in a man of the match display in the 2018 League Cup final win over Arsenal.

However, it is perhaps his thunderbolt at home to Leicester in 2019, which again proved vital as we edged towards another title success, that provides the defining image of his City career. Nothing will ever beat the 'Agueroooo' moment for sheer ecstasy, but this came pretty close.

"There have been many important contributors to Manchester City's renaissance, but arguably none are more important than Vincent Kompany," Khaldoon Al Mubarak said in his tribute to Kompany when the defender decided to call time on his City career just hours after completing a clean-sweep of domestic honours as we lifted the 2019 FA Cup. "He defines the essence of the club. For a decade he has been the lifeblood, the soul, and beating heart of a supremely talented squad."

Words of that magnitude are needed to define Kompany's impact. His influence went far beyond the pitch; he was a captain, leader and statesman, representing City with distinction throughout his time here – a figurehead almost impossible to replace.

Kompany left the club having won four Premier League titles, two FA Cups, four League Cups and two Community Shields. In total, he played 360 times, scoring 20 goals.

His legacy, though, lives on. He set new standards and demanded more. Few, if any, have done more to turn City into a winning machine.

PABLO ZABALETA

Of all the players featured in this book, the one who epitomises the term "fans' favourite" is undoubtedly Pablo Zabaleta, a true idol who, during a nine-year stay at City, played 333 times and gave every ounce of energy he could muster to help us become a successful football club.

He joined as a 23-year-old from Espanyol in 2008. For his first few seasons at City, he was used in multiple positions across defence and midfield, but he became a right-back specialist under Roberto Mancini, forcing his way into our starting XI towards the end of the 2011-12 season as we won the Premier League title.

Zabaleta, the model professional and manager's dream, had nailed down a place in City's best XI and the following season saw him handed the vice captaincy, win City's Player of the Year award and earn a new contract.

The improvement he had undergone since joining the club was incredible; he had become a player City relied on and would remain so until his final day.

"When I came to Manchester, it was a different club and a different era – but after nine years, look where we are," he said in his final City interview. "This is something that makes me very proud. I have tried to give my all for the team and the club and this is something fans appreciate."

Was Zabaleta the most technically gifted player we've had during the last decade? Not by any means, as he would be the first to admit. But can any other player we've had during that period claim to have maximised their ability in quite the same way? It seems unlikely.

"It's been a privilege to work with him," former City assistant manager

Brian Kidd says. "I've been very lucky in my career but they don't come any better than Pablo Zabaleta. Forget about him as a footballer but as a person – fantastic. I can't say enough good things about him."

His departure was difficult to deal with. Our fans struggled to comprehend life without Zaba, having placed him alongside more gilded players in their list of City greats. His farewell inside the Etihad after his final game, a 3-1 win over West Brom, was an emotional occasion that left very few dry eyes in the house.

He captured hearts and minds – and embodied the spirit of the terraces. A fighter who knew only one way of playing: to give his all every single time he went out on to the pitch. Zabaleta started life at City as a Mr Versatile but left widely regarded as the finest Premier League right-back of the 2010s. To achieve that took dedication, professionalism and sheer hard work.

"He represents a lot of the values that the people of Manchester look up to," Vincent Kompany says. "Very simple things but, you know, hard work, commitment, passion – all these things that you associate with people from Manchester."

Often, there is a single image that defines a player's time at a particular club. For Pablo, it is perhaps the one of him kissing the badge and staring passionately into the away end after scoring a vital goal away at Roma in 2014, a coming-of-age performance for City in the Champions League.

That's how City fans will remember Zabaleta, as a player who cared as much as they did about our football club and represented us with distinction throughout his time here.

GARETH BARRY

As underrated footballers in the modern game go, few can match Gareth Barry, a player whose understated qualities saw him carve out a vital role in the Manchester City team that ended decades of hurt and brought success to a long-suffering fanbase.

In fact, for a generation of City supporters, Barry became a barometer of how much a fellow football fan knew about the game. If they were aware of his tactical acumen, his intelligence and his metronomic passing ability, and understood he was a vital component in keeping City well oiled, they clearly watched the game in detail. If instead they reached for cliches and wrote Barry off as someone without star quality, they clearly didn't grasp the nuances of football.

Barry was a superb signing for City, a player whose mettle was obvious from before he had even signed. Having turned down Liverpool in favour of a move to City, he received significant criticism from the national press. But rather than shirk the challenge, he faced it head on.

Brian Marwood, at the time City's Director of Football and a key architect in signing Barry, picks up the story.

"We were in a car going to the medical and we had TalkSPORT on and people were absolutely slaughtering Gareth (for) choosing Manchester City over Liverpool," Marwood recalls.

"It was: 'He's only gone for the money and he's no ambition' and 'Who are City compared to Liverpool?'

"And I remember saying: 'You want to turn this off?' and Gareth said: 'No, I want to listen to this.'

"I said: 'Why do you want to listen to this?'

"He said: 'Because I'm going to prove these people wrong. Actually, Liverpool are offering me more money, but I want to come here because you've sold me about a vision, you've sold me about trying to create history. I'm really determined to make this work.'"

He completed his transfer from Aston Villa on 2 June, 2009. "Gareth is widely acknowledged as one of the top midfielders in the Premier League," the then City manager Mark Hughes said after the move was confirmed.

If there were any doubts among the City fans about Hughes' assertion they were soon allayed. Barry rarely gave the ball away, always seemed to be in the right place at the right time and could contribute both defensively and offensively.

Like most players at City at the time, he further improved once Roberto Mancini took charge, becoming the fulcrum of City's midfield and widely considered to be a key architect of City's 2011 FA Cup success and our 2012 Premier League title win.

Barry played 175 times for City, scoring eight goals. Across his storied career, he was capped 53 times by England and remains the Premier League's all-time leading appearance maker with a remarkable 653 appearances.

Given the criticism he received when he made the move to City, how does he feel it worked out?

"Looking back now I couldn't have made a better decision," Barry says. "I played with some fantastic players. I had a great four years at City and wish I could have had a couple more."

The City fans summed up his importance and impact best with their terrace chant set to the tune of a Morrissey classic: "You're the one for me, Barry!"

CARLOS TEVEZ

The impact Carlos Tevez had at Manchester City should not be underestimated.

City were looking to disrupt the established elite when he arrived in the summer of 2009. We needed a winner, someone world-class in the final third with drive and determination that would raise the collective level to new heights.

Tevez's arrival would help light the blue touch paper – the right man at the right time in our evolution.

After spending two years at Manchester United, he turned down a contract offer at Old Trafford to join City's revolution.

It was a transfer that sent shockwaves through the Premier League, with the famous 'Welcome to Manchester' banner a significant cultural moment. City weren't just signing one of the world's best forwards, the club was sending a message to its rivals that we will compete with anyone to bring in the required quality for us to challenge at the top of the game. The banner, displayed on Deansgate in Manchester city centre, symbolised City's new-found ambition and the shifting power dynamic at the top of the English game.

Born in Fuerte Apache, a tough Buenos Aires suburb, Tevez was a product of his environment. Few players in world football displayed the same tenacity and will to win.

"I'll always keep fighting during games and I've no doubt that is due to my upbringing as a kid in Fuerte Apache," Tevez told the official City magazine back in 2010. "Some days you would find it hard to find something to eat, even a piece of bread. It was a day-to-day struggle, and you would have to fight to get what you needed. I suppose I play like that on the pitch, too."

It was that desire that saw him selected as captain for the 2010-11 season, a campaign in which he produced his best football for City. We were nowhere near the finished article, but Tevez's brilliance would often elevate our level.

We ended the 2010-11 season with the FA Cup – our first trophy in 35 years. Tevez had returned from injury just days before the final. It was fitting he was involved in a game of that magnitude, given the key role he had played throughout the campaign.

"In his first two years, he carried the team on his back," Joleon Lescott told ManCity.com. "We won a lot of games by one goal, and that was down to Carlos."

The following season saw him banished from the squad for six months after refusing to come on as a substitute in a game away at Bayern Munich.

But Tevez's return in February gave City added impetus as we chased our first league title in 44 years. His first game was against Chelsea in March and saw him come off the bench to produce a brilliant assist for Sami Nasri's late winner, but it was perhaps his hat-trick at Carrow Road in a 6-1 win that best exemplifies his impact.

He may not be the best player who has played for City during the last decade, or the most enduring. But he was vitally important, a man who did more than most to create our winning mentality.

JOLEON LESCOTT

Every successful side needs a solid centre-back pairing on which to build, and in the summer of 2009, City were in need of a left-footed option to help solidify our backline as we looked to become contenders for major silverware.

Joleon Lescott was the chosen one, arriving from Everton where he had impressed since joining from Wolves three years earlier. "The way this club is moving on, I'm really looking forward to being a part of that," Lescott said in his first interview as a City player.

He was right to be excited. City were going places.

He partnered Kolo Touré initially and it wasn't until February 2011, with Roberto Mancini in charge, he was paired alongside Vincent Kompany. Those two would gel almost immediately and go on to form the bedrock of our 2011 FA Cup and 2012 Premier League successes, rooting out years of underachievement and changing the mentality of the football club forever.

Lescott may not have been one of the club's top stars, but he recognised the importance of creating partnerships on the pitch. "There was Yaya [Touré], Sergio [Aguero] and Vinny that were gonna play," Lescott says. "So, if you were their best partner, you were gonna play. I knew that."

"Joleon is an amazing centre-half, one of the cleverest I have played with," Kompany said in 2011 as their partnership was flourishing. "He makes it easy for you because he listens and he gives good advice."

Lescott played in every one of our FA Cup matches as we lifted our first piece of silverware in 35 years and was exceptional in both the semi-final and final as City's tight defence provided a platform for success. By the end of that season – with a trophy in the bag and Champions League qualification secured – it was clear he was our best option to play alongside Kompany, whose status in the game was increasing all the time.

The following season was Lescott's best at the club. He was outstanding, a beacon of consistency as City found a new gear and became Premier League champions, with his winning goal at Aston Villa in mid-February a crucial moment en route to the title.

He was arguably England's best player at Euro 2012, but he returned to City and was told by Mancini he would no longer be first choice, a decision that still baffles Lescott now. Matija Nastasic was brought in and became a regular and Lescott's time at City was never the same again, his wings unexpectedly clipped as his career appeared to be in the ascendency.

Manuel Pellegrini joined in the summer of 2013 and a new era was ushered in. The 2013-14 season was to be Lescott's last at City. He played just 10 Premier League games as we won the title again and left in the summer to join West Brom.

In total, he made 160 appearances for City, winning two Premier League titles, an FA Cup and a League Cup.

A superb defender who gave everything to help City become a side capable of winning silverware, Lescott will always be held in high regard. He now appears as a guest on the club's Matchday Live show aired across its digital channels and is a regular pundit for BT Sport.

"There was Yaya, Sergio and Vinny that were gonna play. So if you were their best partner, you were gonna play. I knew that"

ROBERTO MANCINI

Appointed as City boss in December 2009, Roberto Mancini replaced Mark Hughes, who had presided over a slow start to the new season, drawing seven matches in succession and leaving with us sixth in the Premier League table.

The media were initially sceptical. Mancini, they felt, wasn't equipped for life in the Premier League and they set about testing the former Italian international's credentials. During the press conference ahead of his first game in charge against Stoke City, one reporter decided to check Mancini's knowledge of the English game. Who played right-back for the visitors? he asked. "Rory Delap," he shot back.

It was insulting to question Mancini's preparation. He was meticulous in his planning and immediately made City harder to beat, bringing pragmatism and organisation to a side that had too often looked cavalier. We ended the 2009/10 season fifth, just one place higher than where the Italian found us, but there had been significant improvements.

The mentality was shifting; Mancini was a force to be reckoned with. He talked of "taking down the banner" at Old Trafford that charted the number of years City hadn't won a trophy and looked ready to fight anyone who tried to stand in our way of silverware. A fanbase riddled with an inferiority complex and a fear everything that could go wrong would go wrong, suddenly had a figurehead who was bold, vocal and suave.

And he was true to his word. Our 2011 FA Cup success saw Mancini deliver on his promise. We beat Manchester United in the semi-final (a seismic day in our metamorphosis from losers to winners), before seeing off Stoke City in the final just days after sealing our first-ever Champions League qualification with a 1-0 win at home to Tottenham.

The negativity had been rooted out. City were now capable of winning trophies. The following season, Mancini memorably added the Premier League title to our trophy cabinet – our first league title in 44 years. En route we beat Manchester United 6-1 at Old Trafford, before finishing the season with six straight wins, culminating in a last-gasp 3-2 victory over Queens Park Rangers to seal the trophy in the most dramatic circumstances imaginable.

Mancini had established a deep, emotional bond with the City fans. It may only have been symbolism, but the relationship was perhaps best exemplified by the blue-and-white scarf he wore at matches. It demonstrated he wasn't simply a manager, but that he was a fan just like us.

Indeed, so important was the scarf to him, he refused to stand on the touchline without it. Back in 2010, with City facing a trip to West Ham United, Mancini realised he had left it back in Manchester. Chris Bailey, at the time the club's Editor-on-Chief, was speedily dispatched to East London to ensure the manager was reacquainted with his lucky scarf in time for kick off.

Mancini left City on May 13, 2013, just two days after defeat to Wigan Athletic in the FA Cup final at Wembley and a year to the day since he had delivered the Premier League title. "Roberto's record speaks for itself, he secured the love and respect of our fans," said chairman Khaldoon Al Mubarak. "He has done as he promised and delivered silverware and success."

It was perhaps time for a change – many of Mancini's relationships had wilted – but there can be no doubt he left an indelible mark on the club.

He turned City into winners and did it with charisma and style, his bond with the fans to this day unbroken.

Forza, Mancini!

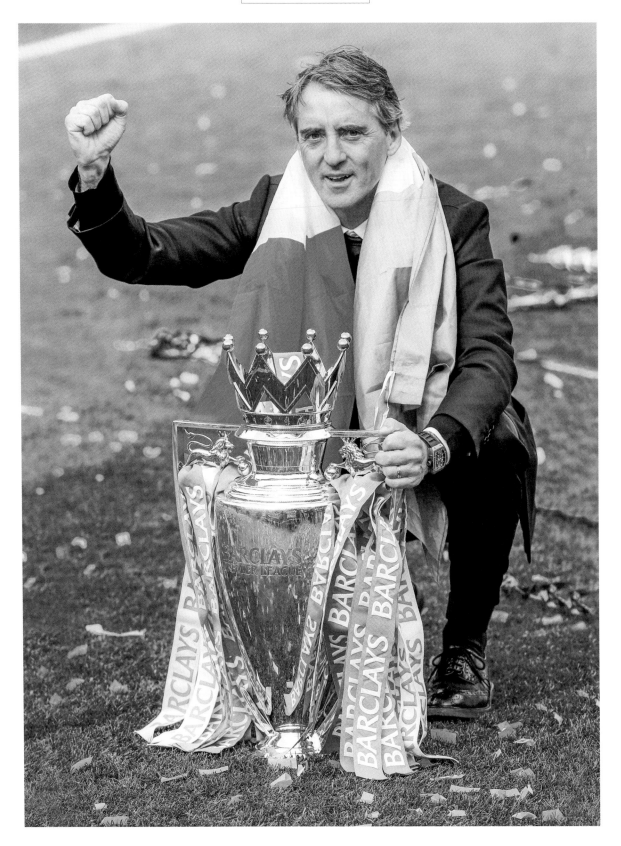

ROBERTO MANCINI
Managerial statistics

Games	191
Won	113
Drawn	38
Lost	40
Goals For	361
Goals against	176
Goals difference	185
Win Percentage %	59.2%
Trophies	3
Games per trophy	63.7
Start date	19/12/2009
End Date	13/05/2013
Total days	1241

YAYA TOURÉ

When Yaya Touré signed from Barcelona in 2010, there were accusations in various quarters he had come for financial, rather than sporting, reasons. Why would someone leave Barcelona, who stood at the pinnacle of the European game, for Manchester City, who hadn't won a trophy for more than three decades?

But Touré took a different view. He saw joining City as an opportunity to create history, to be the catalyst for change and propel the club into a totally different direction. City wanted to disrupt the established order and Touré felt he could help lead the charge.

It was a brave decision but when he left City eight years later, having won three Premier League titles, an FA Cup and three League Cups, as well as being named in the PFA Team of the Year twice, his motives could no longer be questioned. The Ivorian was a force of nature, a player who, at his best, was genuinely unplayable and is now widely considered one of English football's recent greats.

Touré possessed every attribute a midfielder needs. A highly intelligent footballer, he had pace and power, could attack and defend, was technically excellent, rarely gave the ball away and regularly produced breath-taking brilliance from set pieces.

But it's perhaps his list of significant goals that offers the best example of his value. Touré was the ultimate big-game player, capable of rising to any occasion and providing decisive moments. Of the 82 goals he scored for City, a significant portion were vital.

He scored the winner in both the semi-final and final of the FA Cup in 2011 as we ended a 35-year wait for silverware. "I was delighted," he says. "When you win trophies, the mentality

changes – you want to live it again. I was so proud."

A year later, he scored twice away at Newcastle United in our penultimate Premier League game, edging us closer to our first league title in 44 years (in the leadup to the game, he even told Joleon Lescott of his premonition he would score two).

His opus was the 2013-14 season when he scored a ridiculous 24 goals in all competitions as we won our first ever league and cup double, including one of the greatest League Cup final goals ever scored, as we beat Sunderland 3-1 at Wembley.

His strike in the win at home to Aston Villa as we closed in on our second title in three years summed up his unique ability, leaving a series of Villa players on the floor as he ran from the halfway line and powered home.

"So, before he breaks away and he scores – oh Yaya Touré I think we should pay him some more!"

His arrival also helped elevate our transfer strategy. Garry Cook, the club's former chief executive, famously convinced David Silva to sign on the proviso Touré would join. It seemed once Yaya was in place, the very best players sat up and took note.

"When I joined, I did some interviews and said I want to leave the club with some big achievements. We made it and it's perfect!" he said in his final City interview in 2018.

"I'm delighted. I've been very focused – and lucky as well, to be honest, because after I came, we had players like Aguero, Silva, Balotelli and Dzeko join the club. We've always been at a good level. Even when we haven't won the league, we've been there challenging.

"The Club has changed a lot. It's my pleasure – I feel I have contributed to something."

DAVID SILVA

In the final seconds of City's seismic 6-1 victory at Old Trafford in 2011, a game emblematic of the shifting power balance in Manchester, David Silva produced a moment of true genius.

With the ball dropping inside the City half, he hit an inch-perfect, half-volley pass that split the United defence wide open and put Edin Dzeko through on goal. It was perfectly weighted, with the Bosnian striker not having to break stride as he steadied himself with a couple of touches before firing home to add the final goal and inflict on United their heaviest defeat at Old Trafford since 1955.

It may only be one split second on a football pitch – one pass in a career of consistent virtuosity – but it is perhaps the archetypal example of Silva's wonderful ability: vision, speed of thought, skill, beauty, technique and audacity all combining at the home of our rivals who had for so long cast a shadow on our existence.

"He's a genuine pleasure to watch," said Colin Bell back in 2019. "When he's on the ball he makes the whole team tick."

Indeed, Bell's assessment perhaps cuts to the heart of why Silva was so good. Headline stats simply do not tell the whole story. It was his constant brilliance in small spaces, his ball retention, his ability to find a pass and his selflessness that made him such a key figure in the club's most successful 10-year period. When he played, City were a slicker machine.

"He's one of the most incredible players in the world playing in the pockets," says Pep Guardiola. "He is a master at that."

> "David Silva is a transformational player. He has put a stamp on the team, on this club, its history and even the Premier League as a whole. In doing so, he has been instrumental to the beautiful football philosophy you see today. He was the start of it"

Silva played 436 times for City, which puts him 10th on our list of all-time appearance makers, and he won four Premier League titles, two FA Cups, five League Cups and three Community Shields. His 70 appearances in European competition is a club record.

"David Silva is a transformational player," club chairman, Khaldoon Al Mubarak, said after Silva played his final game for City in 2020. "He has put a stamp on the team, on this club, its history and even the Premier League as a whole. In doing so, he has been instrumental to the beautiful football philosophy you see today. He was the start of it."

It was a fitting tribute from the chairman, but perhaps an even more succinct appraisal came from the great Xavi. "He's a spectacular footballer," the Spain and Barcelona legend said when interviewed for the CITY+ documentary Made in Gran Canaria.

David Silva. The understated genius whose artistry helped redefine City's aesthetic.

MARIO BALOTELLI

A maverick. A one-off. Unique.

There were many words used to describe Mario Balotelli during his time at City – not all of them complimentary – but one thing we can say with confidence is there's no one quite like the Italian.

Roberto Mancini signed him in the summer of 2010 and it became obvious very quickly we were dealing with a player who was different.

During a troubled-but-sometimes-brilliant three-year spell in Manchester, the mercurial striker scored a goal with his shoulder; struggled to get a bib on before a game against Dynamo Kiev; fronted a firework safety campaign after a friend set his bathroom alight; was hastily substituted after pirouetting and miscuing a backheel when clean through on goal in a friendly and was sent off in a crucial game at Arsenal that threatened to derail our 2012 title bid.

But in amongst the madness, mishaps and misdemeanours was a fine talent. It's why Mancini persevered for so long. Other players were not afforded such luxuries, but Balotelli, in his eyes, was worth the effort.

His life and career had been complicated. He was seriously ill with a chronic intestinal condition as a baby and fostered as a three-year-old after being given up for adoption by his Ghanaian parents, who could not support him financially through his health issues. As he came through the ranks at Inter Milan, Juventus fans hung a banner with the message "a Negro cannot be Italian," just one example of racism he has had to deal with during his professional career. Jose Mourinho, who took over from Mancini at Inter Milan, marginalised him after what he saw as disrespect in a training session, describing him as "a nobody."

But Mancini had known Balotelli when the striker was a 15-year-old in Inter's youth system and gave him the chance to play in Serie A. There was almost a paternal bond. He wanted to unlock his clear potential. "If Mancini wasn't at City, I don't think I would ever have come," Balotelli says.

His first season saw him score 10 goals in 28 appearances, with an outstanding display in the FA Cup semi-final win over Manchester United his highlight.

The 2011-12 season was perhaps his best in a City shirt. He scored 20 goals in 40 matches and showed flashes of pure genius, his most crucial moment the assist for Sergio Aguero's winner against QPR in the final game of the 2011-12 season. His best performance came in the 6-1 win at Old Trafford, as he bullied the United backline, scored twice and revealed the now world famous 'Why Always Me?' t-shirt.

That summer, he impressed at the Euros with Italy, bagging a brace in the semi-final win over Germany. City fans expected that to signal further improvement, for Balotelli to take his performance level and consistency to the next level, but he failed to kick on. He played just 20 times the following campaign, 12 of which came from the bench, scoring three goals, with Mancini preferring to use his more reliable striking resources.

He joined AC Milan in January 2013, weeks after a training ground altercation with Mancini. "We love Mario, but he had this big chance to go back to Italy," Mancini said.

It ended one of the more colourful chapters of City's new era. He was flawed and, perhaps, too much trouble. But Balotelli was a hugely talented player who contributed to our success and left memories that will last a lifetime.

When everything came together – technique, pace, power, hold-up ability and intelligence - he was unplayable. Unfortunately, those occasions were too fleeting.

EDIN DZEKO

Edin Dzeko, the Bosnian Diamond.

For a striker who arrived at City to little fanfare – and one who was always surrounded by players who were seen as more talented – he left a huge mark on the club during his four-and-a-half years, scoring 72 goals in 189 games and winning two Premier League titles, an FA Cup and a League Cup.

He made a slow start, in truth. He joined during the January transfer window of 2011 and played 21 matches before the end of the season, scoring just six goals.

Two of them, however, were crucial, the first indications he was a man with an ability to score important goals.

The first was a late equaliser in an FA Cup fourth round match away at Notts County. City looked to be heading out until Dzeko's tap in averted disaster and forced a replay, which we won 5-0 before going on to win the competition for the first time since 1969.

And the second saw him score the winner away at Blackburn, a result that left Champions League qualification in our own hands with five matches of the season remaining.

He flew out of the blocks the following campaign and really found his groove. He scored six in his first three league games, including a four-goal haul away at Spurs as City produced a statement win at White Hart Lane. He then scored twice at Old Trafford in our famous 6-1 win over Manchester United during a run of seven goals in eight matches in the autumn. City were ready to make an assault on the title and Dzeko was spearheading our charge.

His ability to score vital goals was in evidence again when he scored the winner at Wigan in January 2012, but

his most important came in the final match of the season. With City losing 2-1 at home to QPR and our title hopes hanging by a thread, Dzeko headed home a late equaliser, paving the way for Sergio Aguero to score the most famous goal in Premier League history and win City our first title in 44 years.

"If you look at Edin's career for Manchester City, the goals he has scored, he has got a lot of heavy goals, goals that are very important," former assistant manager David Platt said in 2012 after Dzeko scored two goals from the bench as City beat West Brom away from home.

Dzeko was central to our 2013-14 season success, too, scoring 26 goals in 48 matches across all competitions, including vital goals against Crystal Palace, Everton and Aston Villa as City won the Premier League and League Cup. Any doubts about his ability were swept away in what was a glorious campaign for the Bosnian, his best in a City shirt by far.

Eventually his time at the Etihad came to an end. He joined Roma in 2015 on a season-long loan before making the deal permanent. He has scored well over 100 goals during his six years in the Italian capital.

However, his bond with the City fans remains strong, with the song recalling the dramatic climax to the 2013-14 season still sung regularly at games – and Dzeko remains a City fan to this day.

"Since I left, I follow every City game in every competition and it's just natural for me because I feel it is still my club, even if I'm not there anymore," he says.

City win five in a row and we're all singing Edin Dzeko!

City 1-0 United

MINDSET SHIFTS ON GLORIOUS DAY AT WEMBLEY

FA Cup semi-final, 16 April 2011

The takeover of Manchester City by the Abu Dhabi United Group, completed in 2008, had promised so much. The new owners were revolutionising the club on and off the field, with the playing squad and support staff improved immeasurably. A platform for a new era of success had been put in place and many observers felt silverware was inevitable.

But given the decades of underachievement and mismanagement that had preceded the acquisition, there was a deep-rooted sense of failure that pervaded City supporters of all ages. 'Cityitis,' a phrase coined by former manager Joe Royle to describe the fear that everything that *could* go wrong *would* go wrong, remained burned into the collective psyche.

Changing that was going to be key if a new era was to truly crystallise. Being hamstrung and held back by past failures wasn't conducive to recasting ourselves and writing a new chapter of success.

Our FA Cup semi-final win over Manchester United was perhaps the most significant moment in altering that mindset. It felt seismic, the kind of win that sees belief and optimism multiply in an instant. In the eyes of many, this was the day everything changed.

We had knocked out Leicester, Notts County, Aston Villa and Reading to reach the final four, but this was a different test. United were closing in on a 19th league title and were the most successful English football club over the previous two decades. Our cross-city rivals who had ridiculed us for so long remained at the forefront of the game; our revival was a work in progress, not yet fully formed.

But City delivered. In one of the most tense, fraught 90 minutes in our history, a single goal separated the sides and booked a return trip to Wembley a month later for the final, ending United's hope of a treble in the process.

Yaya Touré scored the winner – the first of a long list of vital goals the Ivorian would deliver during his time at the club. Michael Carrick gave the ball away, Touré pounced and went past two, before slotting the ball home between Edwin van der Sar's legs. Cue delirium in one half of Wembley.

Paul Scholes was sent off late on for a lunge on Pablo Zabaleta, with City convincing winners in the end. Given the absence of Carlos Tevez, our most inspirational forward player and the team's talisman, the ease with which City won was surprising. City were the more inventive, expansive side and Mario Balotelli, who led the line on his own, was superb.

When the final whistle sounded, the roar from the City fans said it all. There was huge excitement about qualifying for our first FA Cup final in 30 years, but, perhaps more pertinently, there was deep relief. After a litany of abject failures that had seen us go 35 years without a piece of silverware, we had gone to Wembley and beaten our biggest rival to move within one win of that elusive trophy.

"I am very happy for our supporters, because they deserve this," Roberto Mancini said afterwards. "It is important to start winning trophies, and I stand by my claim that if we win the FA Cup this year we can try for the title next season.

"This could be a turning point for us, but it is important to remember there is another game to win. I think we can go on from this to win the FA Cup and secure a top-four finish."

Mancini's words proved incredibly prophetic.

It was the day we started to believe – and the day the balance of power in English football began to alter.

City 1-0 Tottenham

FIRST-EVER CHAMPIONS LEAGUE QUALIFICATION SECURED

10 May 2011

City qualified for the Champions League for the first time after a hard-fought 1-0 win over Tottenham guaranteed a top-four finish with two matches of the 2010/11 season remaining.

And in an incredible twist of irony, it was a Peter Crouch own goal that secured victory – almost 12 months to the day after his winner at the Etihad had denied City the chance to play in Europe's elite knock-out competition.

The pressure on City to qualify was significant, and that was reflected by the crowd inside Eastlands who were tense and nervous throughout.

Tottenham dominated for long periods, but Mancini had made City difficult to break down, and the solitary goal, scored after half an hour of the game, was enough to see his team over the line.

Joe Hart's exceptional stop to deny Steven Pienaar early in the second half proved crucial, with the City goalkeeper once again underlining his growing importance to the side.

And the game was also the latest example of David Silva's quality. After a difficult first few months in English football, the Spanish midfielder was now fully adjusted to the physical demands of the Premier League and his creative genius was in full flow. Few players could play in the pockets quite like Silva, with his ability to thread a pass a key facet of City's attacking style.

After the game, Vincent Kompany described City's qualification as "a milestone".

"Everybody's happy," he said. "It's a milestone for this club.

"I don't think people imagine how far we've come. It takes a lot to catch the Premier League teams who have been in the top four for a long time and we're there now.

"We have the feeling that from this stage on we can build and challenge for the title."

Kompany was right – this was a significant juncture in City's journey to the top of the English game. Having improved drastically under the guidance of Roberto Mancini – and with the club strengthening in every area off the pitch, too – dining at Europe's top table would now allow City access to the very best players. The opportunity to join such a forward-thinking club who were competing with the best teams in Europe was an enticing mix for any prospective new signing.

This was exactly where the club's owners wanted to be.

It was also the perfect boost ahead of the FA Cup final against Stoke City at Wembley, a game that presented City with a chance to end our 35-year wait for silverware.

City 1-0 Stoke City
35-YEAR WAIT FOR SILVERWARE ENDS WITH FA CUP WIN
14 May 2011

We will take that banner down," Roberto Mancini said in January 2010, shortly after his appointment as City boss, referring to the giant display at Old Trafford charting the number of years City had gone without winning silverware. "This is the last year it will be displayed because we will win."

Mancini had to wait a little longer than he predicted, but a glorious 1-0 win over Stoke City in the 2011 FA Cup final saw him deliver on his bold prediction. Yaya Toure, the hero of the semi-final victory over United, struck the winner again, powering home with his left foot 16 minutes from time; an emphatic finish from a player on his way to becoming one of the club's most iconic players. "I just love Wembley," the Ivorian said afterwards.

This was City's fifth FA Cup success from nine final appearances, adding to the victories secured in 1904, 1934, 1956 and 1969.

It was a thoroughly deserved win too. City were dominant, and only a fine display from Stoke keeper Thomas Sorensen had kept Mancini's men at bay for so long, with his first-half saves from Carlos Tevez and Mario Balotelli keeping his side in the game.

It was fitting Tevez started the game, with his cameo four days earlier against Tottenham his first involvement after a month out. He had been a vital signing, often raising City's level with his leadership and tireless work ethic. The Argentine had been a driving force throughout the season and deserved to play a major role in the showpiece final.

Our FA Cup campaign had started with a 2-2 third round draw at Leicester in January, a match played against a backdrop of red and black scarves in the away end as the City fans saluted one of the club's greats. Neil Young's cancer had been diagnosed as terminal towards the end of 2010 and our supporters wanted to send a positive message to one of our most popular but unassuming figures.

Young had scored the winning goal at Wembley when City had last won the FA Cup, way back in 1969. Tragically, he passed away in February 2011 and did not get to see the class of 2011 bring the trophy back home after City had overcome Leicester in a replay and then seen off Notts County (again after a replay), Aston Villa, Reading and United before the Stoke showpiece.

The full-time whistle saw scenes of euphoria across one half of Wembley. The City fans, who had for so long been starved of success, were joyous. This was an outpouring of emotion 35 years in the making.

Liam Wright, a Seasoncard holder for 22 years, says: "It was the first time I'd seen us win anything, so after the game you didn't know what to do! I was a novice when it came to celebrating a trophy. It was a weight

off our shoulders. When the final whistle went, it was jubilation but also a lot of relief that we hadn't messed up the chance to win."

Gazing at the stands, Vincent Kompany, whose performances were getting steadily more influential, said he felt "the first brick" towards success had now been laid.

"Look at what it means to our fans - it's been 35 years. It's just unbelievable," the skipper told CityTV afterwards.

"In my opinion, this is just the first of many trophies to come in the future. We've laid the first brick, now we can build a house.

"We knew Stoke would make it hard. All credit to them, they kept the fight going until the last minute, but if you look at the chances, we deserved to win.

"This is how far we've come. If this isn't a step forward, I don't know what is."

Coming just four days after qualifying for the Champions

League for the first time, City were now writing thrilling new chapters in the club's history, fulfilling the promises made by the new owners after acquiring the club three years earlier.

It was City's first trophy since winning the 1976 League Cup, when Tony Book's side beat Newcastle 2-1 thanks to goals from Peter Barnes and Dennis Tueart. Given the quality of the squad City had then, no one could have predicted the long, arduous wait for the club's next success.

"I'd last seen City win a trophy in 1976," says Andy MacNab, a lifelong City fan. "After that – nothing!

"In 1989 my son James was born and that was at a time when City went through turmoil. He was born into a family that was half red. I always wondered whether United's success and the catastrophe of a club we were, would he want to switch?

"He never did. He stuck with

us. And when we won the FA Cup in 2011, it was without doubt the most emotional I had ever been at a football game. James had never seen us win anything. To be there with him that day was the most emotional moment I've had as a City fan."

"I am happy for the fans, they deserved to win this Cup - for a long time they didn't win," a proud Mancini said. "My feeling is good, but it's important that they feel good [too]."

Midfielder Nigel De Jong, a beaten World Cup finalist 10 months earlier, dedicated the victory to all the fans who had pushed the side over the line.

"The feeling is unbelievable," he said. "We've worked so hard to win this FA Cup, and this was for all our fans. The city will be blue for a long time!

"We deserved it because we dominated from the first minute, though they came back with their set pieces. I missed out on a World Cup

medal in the summer, but I'll happily take this at the moment."

With qualification for the Champions League secured and a glorious FA Cup victory to boot, City had enjoyed a perfect four days – the platform for further success well and truly put down. "Our target was to go to the Champions League and win something and my dream has come true," Toure said.

Our preseason objectives had been met and, crucially, a new winning mentality had been installed. "You ask Roberto which of the trophies was the best while he was at Inter and he will say it was the first Italian Cup because that is what gave the dressing room that winning mentality," assistant manager David Platt pointed out. "What nobody can take away from the players is that they have won something."

Sure enough, just two days after the game at Wembley, the banner at Old Trafford was quietly removed.

SERGIO AGUERO

Sergio Aguero left Manchester City in the summer of 2021 after 10 years at the club, a glittering period which had seen him win 15 major trophies.

Starting with one of the great Premier League debuts and culminating in a cameo appearance in our first-ever Champions League final, Aguero scored 260 goals in 390 games for City, establishing himself as our greatest-ever goalscorer and one of the finest players to ever wear our shirt.

Outside of City circles, he will always be remembered for his goal in the final game of the 2011/12 season – the ultimate climax to a league campaign that sealed our first title in 44 years, a script that would have been rejected out of hand by every Hollywood executive on the grounds it was too far-fetched. It's a moment etched in the mind of every City fan.

"It is the best memory that I will ever have in my head," Aguero said when discussing 93:20 ahead of his final appearance at the Etihad, a 5-0 win over Everton that saw him score twice.

"I don't think it will happen again in another country or in this one. It's not something that can be repeated."

But his time at City encompassed so much more. During his decade at the Etihad, he earned a reputation as not only a Manchester City great but a legend of English football.

He has the best goals-per-minute ratio in Premier League history, scoring one every 108 minutes. His nearest challengers, Thierry Henry and Harry Kane, are on a goal every 122 minutes.

He sits fourth on the list of all-time leading Premier League goalscorers with 184 (no foreign player has ever scored more) and bagged more Premier League hat-tricks than any other player (12).

"Sergio's contribution to Manchester City over the last 10 years cannot be overstated. His legend will be indelibly etched into the memories of everyone who loves the Club"

Quite simply, he was a phenomenon for City, a player with such unique quality in front goal.

In March 2021, as his summer departure was confirmed, City Chairman Khaldoon Al Mubarak revealed a statue of the City striker had been commissioned to stand alongside those of Sergio's former team-mates David Silva and Vincent Kompany.

"Sergio's contribution to Manchester City over the last 10 years cannot be overstated," Khaldoon Al Mubarak said. "His legend will be indelibly etched into the memories of everyone who loves the Club and maybe even in those who simply love football.

"It gives me great pleasure to announce that we will be commissioning an artist to create a statue of Sergio to live at the Etihad Stadium alongside the ones under construction for Vincent and David."

It's the least the club could do for a player who helped transform City into perennial winners. Few players, if any, have contributed more to our decade of success.

City 4-0 Swansea City

AGUERO MARKS DEBUT WITH BLISTERING CAMEO

15 August 2011

Has a debut ever provided such an accurate precursor to a player's time at a club?

Just two-and-a-half weeks after signing for City, Sergio Aguero began warming up ahead of a 30-minute cameo at home to Swansea City. Few inside the Etihad could have imagined the impact he would have.

Having gone in at half-time at 0-0, with Swansea goalkeeper Michel Vorm in fine form, City were 1-0 up when Aguero came on with half an hour remaining after Edin Dzeko had given us a 58th-minute lead.

The Argentine, signed from Atletico Madrid, immediately gave City a new edge after replacing Nigel De Jong, scoring twice and assisting David Silva to help seal a fine 4-0 win. It was one of the finest debuts in Premier League history, joining the likes of Jurgen Klinsmann (Tottenham v Sheffield Wednesday, 1994) and Fabrizio Ravanelli (Middlesbrough v Liverpool, 1996) in the pantheon of iconic first appearances in English football.

He scored his first seven minutes after coming on, a simple back-post tap-in from close range, finishing a fine low ball across the box from Micah Richards.

"How many goals might he get in a sky blue shirt?" Sky Sports co-commentator Alan Smith postulated as Aguero celebrated. No one could have predicted this was the first of the 260 that would see him become our all-time leading goalscorer.

Three minutes later, he turned provider, chasing down Steven Caulker and forcing a miskick, before flicking the ball over Vorm's head and impudently volleying it back over his shoulder to Silva, who finished expertly. It was a moment of instinctive genius from Aguero; the kind observers of English football would soon become accustomed to.

And in the 90th minute, he sent the City fans into delirium with a sensational strike from 30 yards, capping a 4-0 win and a memorable debut display that sent excitement in East Manchester skyrocketing. It was the most emphatic of finishes, buried deep into the far corner of Vorm's goal.

Perhaps the most surprising element of the performance was the fact Aguero wasn't yet match fit, having participated in the Copa America and missed preseason with City.

"You could see straight away that he was special," Vorm said in an interview with ManCity.com in May 2021. "I had just flown in to join the club a few days earlier and we played City on a Monday night and in truth, it was a bit of a blur because so much happened."

It was a special performance showcasing Aguero's talents: a poacher's finish from close range, a moment of improvised brilliance and a blockbuster long-range effort hit with incredible power. The complete package.

A new City hero was born.

"Sergio is a photocopy of Romario, they are the same player," Roberto Mancini said afterwards. "I think he needs to recover as he only finished the Copa America three weeks ago.

"He needs another two to three weeks to be 100%, maybe. For me he's a fantastic striker, young, and he's going to be a fantastic player for us."

It was an accurate description. With his low centre of gravity and superb balance, as well as pace, power and stocky build, there were more than shades of the great Brazilian in Aguero's style.

But Aguero would go on to carve out his own unique career at City, this 30-minute masterclass against Swansea offering a mere glimpse of what was to come.

SAMIR NASRI

There are few players in City's recent history who could retain possession as well as Samir Nasri. With his close control, low centre of gravity and wonderful skill and ability, getting the ball off him sometimes appeared an impossible task for opposition defenders. He was a fine player, an entertainer armed with a fiercely competitive edge.

He arrived at City in 2011 having enjoyed a superb season at Arsenal. He had been electric for the North Londoners, earning a spot in the 2010-11 PFA Team of the Year after scoring 15 times in 46 games across all competitions that season.

"Arsenal have good fans but not that

> "City fans are really passionate. When we played against City, the crowd was amazing. That's what I want"

passionate since they moved from Highbury," Nasri said upon signing. "City fans are really passionate. When we played against City, the crowd was amazing. That's what I want."

If those words weren't enough to get City fans onside, his debut most certainly was. He created four goals as City beat Tottenham 5-1 at White Hart Lane, sending a message of title intent in the process. As City debuts go, this was right up there with the very best.

Nasri and Sergio Aguero were seen as the final pieces of Roberto Mancini's jigsaw and so it proved. We ended the season as Premier League champions, with Nasri clocking up 46 appearances across all competitions. He was central to our success; his late winner against Chelsea with

10 matches of the league season remaining proving vital.

The Frenchman further flourished under Manuel Pellegrini and was central to our league and cup double of 2013-14. He produced a sensational display in the 4-1 win over Manchester United early in the season, bamboozling Chris Smalling in the build up to Aguero's opener, swinging in the corner that led to the second, playing a fine pass in the lead up to the third and, just for good measure, scoring with a volley at the far post for our fourth. It was an instrumental derby display.

His quite brilliant outside-of-the-boot strike in our 3-1 win over Sunderland in the Carabao Cup final at Wembley was perhaps his finest moment, and he scored in our final-day victory over West Ham United that sealed our second title win in three seasons. It capped a wonderful campaign for a player often questioned in the media.

"There are no words to explain our feelings right now," Nasri said after sealing the 2013-14 Premier League title. "Maybe in an hour or two we will really feel it."

Ultimately, injuries hampered Nasri's remaining time at City and he spent Pep Guardiola's first season in charge on loan at Sevilla before moving permanently to Turkish side Antalyaspor the following year.

There remains a feeling of 'what if?' about Nasri's City career. Surely, with his talent, had he avoided the injuries that saw his career stall, he could have excelled under Guardiola.

Even with those regrets, however, Nasri's time at City was excellent. A truly quality player who regularly lit up matches and was instrumental to our success early in the decade.

Tottenham 1-5 City

DZEKO HITS FOUR AS CITY SEND OUT CLEAR MESSAGE TO RIVALS

28 August 2011

City's 100% start to the 2011-12 season continued with a blistering performance away at Tottenham.

Edin Dzeko scored four as he produced arguably his finest display for City, and Sergio Aguero bagged the other to make it three wins from three in the Premier League.

It felt like a new era of attack-minded football was being ushered in, with the pragmatism Roberto Mancini introduced immediately after his appointment in 2009 being replaced with a more ferocious, free-wheeling style.

Key to that transition was Samir Nasri, a summer signing from Arsenal who made his debut at White Hart Lane and produced a virtuoso display, setting up three of City's five goals.

"We bought Samir right before the game and everyone knew about his quality and what he could bring to this team, and he did exactly that," Dzeko told mancity.com in 2020.

It took Nasri 34 minutes to make an impact, playing a one-two with Aguero before crossing beautifully for Dzeko to open the scoring from close range.

It was 2-0 seven minutes later when Nasri played an exquisite, lofted pass in to Dzeko, whose header to finish was excellent.

City were turning on the style and Yaya Touré provided Dzeko with a tap-in to make it 3-0, as the striker completed a 21-minute perfect hat-trick – left foot, right foot, header – in what was turning out to be a dream afternoon for the Bosnian.

Aguero soon got in on the act, scoring his first away goal for the club, Nasri making it three assists with an outside-of-the-boot pass to release the Argentine, who then beat Michael Dawson with ease before firing past Brad Friedel.

A Younes Kaboul header saw Spurs pull one back on 68 minutes, but Dzeko got his fourth – "probably one of my best goals for City" – when he played a one-two with Gareth Barry before bending the ball brilliantly into the top corner with a first-time finish deep into injury time.

In the Spurs midfield that day was Luka Modric, one of the most respected players in the Premier League at the time and a man who would go on to win the Ballon d'Or in 2018, breaking the Cristiano Ronaldo-Lionel Messi duopoly. Alongside him were Rafael van der Vaart, Gareth Bale and Niko Kranjcar. This was a team full of quality who were completely overshadowed by the skill and ingenuity on display from City.

Dzeko, who had scored in each of City's opening two matches, was on six Premier League goals for the season already, having managed two in 15 the previous season after signing in January. "It's something fantastic to have after three games nine points and I have scored six goals," he said after the game. "It's amazing. We have nine points from three games – it's perfect, but it's a long way until the end of the season."

The excitement caused by City's FA Cup triumph and first ever Champions League qualification three months earlier increased after three wins from three at the start of the new campaign. To dismantle a fine Spurs side with such ease demonstrated City's growing belief and sent a message to the rest of the Premier League. This was a side with tremendous balance, displaying power, poise and class, capable of ending the club's 44-year wait for a league title.

City 1-1 Napoli
KOLAROV STRIKES ON RETURN TO EUROPE'S BIGGEST FOOTBALL STAGE
14 September 2011

It had been a long wait but on **14 September, 2011 we made our Champions League debut, hosting Napoli at the Etihad Stadium.**

After setbacks, heartache and being written off in some quarters, we had finally arrived on the biggest stage, facing a side who finished third in Serie A the previous campaign.

With our form in the Premier League outstanding (we had won our first four matches, scoring 15 goals along the way), it was time to test ourselves in a different environment. European football is a more technical and tactical affair, a separate challenge from the pace and power of the Premier League.

In truth, City found it hard to adapt. Roberto Mancini called for a quick start in his programme notes, but with the Italians well organised and technically proficient, capable of sitting back, absorbing pressure and hitting City on the break, we struggled to impose our attacking game.

Pretty much every Italian football stereotype was true of Napoli. They were streetwise, tactically well drilled and superb at the back – their game plan executed superbly.

City had the majority of the play – 68% possession, to be precise – but unlike the dismantling of Swansea, Wigan and Tottenham in recent Premier League games, Mancini's side could not turn that dominance into a tidal wave of goals. It felt like a crash course in the realities of Champions League football.

Ezequiel Lavezzi hit the bar for Napoli and Marek Hamsik saw his goal-bound effort blocked by Vincent Kompany. For City, both Yaya Touré and Sergio Aguero hit the frame of the goal.

Edinson Cavani broke the deadlock with 69 minutes played, finishing off a fine counter-attacking move from the Italians.

But six minutes later, Aleksandr Kolarov powered home a fine free-kick that left Morgan De Sanctis rooted to the spot and ensured our Champions League bow ended in a respectable draw.

It was our first goal in Europe's premier knock-out competition since Tony Coleman netted in a 2-1 defeat to Fenerbahce in the first round of the 1968/69 European Cup. Back then, visionary coach Malcolm Allison proclaimed City would "terrify Europe," only to fall at the first hurdle.

Forty-three years is a long time, but we were now back among the elite; our first time since the competition's rebrand in 1992. Allison wasn't there to enjoy it, but he would no doubt have been delighted to see his former club hold their own against wily opposition.

Ultimately, though, Group A proved too difficult for City in our maiden Champions League campaign. We won three and drew one of our six group matches, with 10 points not enough to advance to the last-16. In a group also containing Villarreal and Bayern Munich, it was a more than respectable return, but the brutal nature of this competition was laid bare. We had to settle for Europa League football instead.

A steep learning curve, but a valuable one on our journey towards becoming one of the best teams in world football.

Manchester United 1-6 City

POWER BALANCE SHIFTS ON HISTORIC DAY AT OLD TRAFFORD

23 October 2011

There have been many memorable occasions in City's recent history, but few can match our win at Old Trafford early in the 2011-12 season.

It had everything. Fierce rivals going head to head, one the current Premier League champions and English football's preeminent side over the previous two decades, the other looking to disrupt the established elite after a much-needed injection of finance and direction.

City fans had been ridiculed by their United counterparts for the best part of 20 years. Our epic failures coupled with United's dominance had seen the two clubs take very different paths. But in recent seasons, City were enjoying something of a renaissance, with our 35-year wait for silverware over and our maiden Champions League qualification secured. Something special appeared to be building, but United remained the team to beat.

City's rapid improvement under new ownership meant this was a battle between the league's two best sides, with the array of talent on show something to behold. For United, the likes of Rio Ferdinand, Wayne Rooney and Nani, and lining up in sky blue, David Silva, Yaya Touré and Sergio Aguero – a galaxy of stars and the best the Premier League had to offer.

That was reflected in the league table. City were top after the first eight matches having dropped just two points, while United sat second, two points further back. The stage was set for a classic.

What happened changed the landscape of English football, with the balance of power in Manchester shifting after a masterclass from Roberto Mancini's side.

United started strongly but Mario Balotelli opened the scoring after 22 minutes, side-footing home first time after James Milner's cut back to the edge of the area. It was a moment of impudent genius, laced with typical Balotelli nonchalance. To celebrate, the Italian pulled his shirt over his head to reveal the famous 'Why Always Me?' t-shirt underneath, an iconic moment that immediately reverberated across the world and is now woven into City's history.

"It was the perfect thing and the perfect time for that perfect individual," says Les Chapman, City's kit manager at the time who had printed the t-shirt. "A lot of the time players would wear compression shirts and they would ask me to print things on them. Mario asked me on the Monday before the game to print something for him and I said it can't be anything controversial or offensive to the United fans. Out of the blue, he just said, 'why always me?' and I knew straight away that was the one!"

"I did it for many reasons," Balotelli says. "But I'll leave it for other people to figure out what it means. I'm sure people can work it out."

Balotelli, sensational throughout, was at the heart of another significant moment early in the second half. Clean through on goal after muscling his way past Jonny Evans to get on the end of Sergio Aguero's perfectly-weighted throughball, the United defender brought Balotelli down as he looked certain to score. United were rightly reduced to ten men and City took complete control of the game thereafter.

Balotelli doubled our lead with a tap in at the far post after fine work from David Silva and Milner inside the United area, and Micah Richards' pinpoint ball across the box was then tapped home by Aguero for our third.

Indeed, this was arguably Richards' best-ever performance in a sky blue shirt, as he produced a sensational display down our right-hand side, shackling United's attacking threats and bombing forward to devastating effect at every opportunity.

"Because I'd been at City for so long, I always played better against United for some reason because I was just more up for the game," Richards says. "I just didn't want to lose. When you're up against the top players and it's a one-on-one battle, I used to love that, 'he's not getting around me today'. Against United, I just upped my game.

"They went down to ten men and Roberto Mancini just said: 'don't go back'. He kept saying goal difference was going to be important at the end of the season."

United pulled one back when Darren Fletcher played a one-two with Javier Hernandez before curling one into the top corner.

But City were cutting through United at will and more goals were inevitable. Edin Dzeko's knee made it four, Silva capped a masterful display by putting the ball through David De Gea's legs for our fifth, before he produced arguably the greatest Premier League assist of all time to set up Dzeko for the sixth deep into stoppage time.

Manchester United 1-6 Manchester City.

To put the scale of the victory into context, this was United's worst home loss since 1955 and the first time they had conceded six at Old Trafford since 1930. It also represented their heaviest Premier League defeat of all time. City had scored six in a Manchester derby for the first time since 1926.

It was a result that reverberated around the football world.

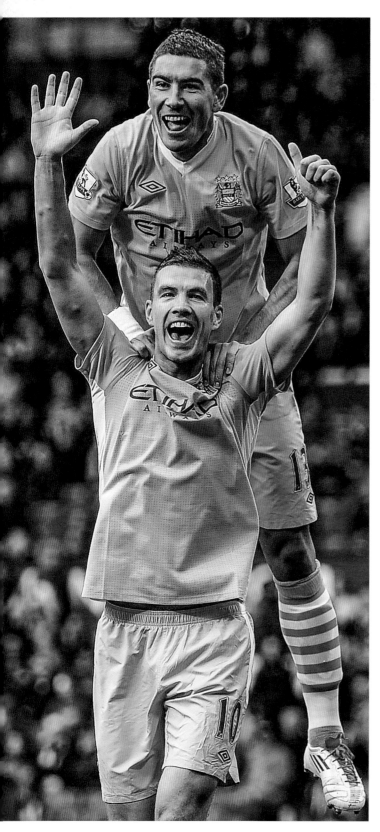

"It was a bad day, no doubt about that," United manager Sir Alex Ferguson said afterwards. "It was our worst ever day.

"The thing that concerns me most was the goals for and against – that was 10 goals of difference today. That was a big blow for us. You never know, goal difference could count."

Mancini, whose gameplan had been executed perfectly, was typically understated in the immediate aftermath, urging caution from his players. "For Manchester City, it will be a great day if we win the Premier League," he said. "We beat a fantastic team like United, but we only took three points."

Of course, City did go on to win the title – with goal difference crucial.

"This is the reason why we won the league," Joleon Lescott says. "If this is 3-1 then we don't win it, it's mad.

"Every game he [Mancini] would say: 'goal difference, goal difference, goal difference'. He said, 'don't stay back, just go and attack'."

The manner of the victory was emphatic. City played with freedom and expression in a stadium that had brought us so much pain. United couldn't live with the pace, power and technical quality in the City side.

"It was a complete performance from the whole team," Silva says. "6-1 against United at Old Trafford. Imagine that. The whole team played so well and it was a historic result."

Richards and Lescott believe this was the day the power balance altered and City became a huge force in English football.

"I don't know if the power was actually shifting until we won 6-1," Richards says. "That was the only time when I thought this was properly shifting."

"It wasn't even shifting, it was shifted," says Lescott.

City 4-0 West Brom

CITY, YOU GOT ME SINGING THE BLUES!

11 April 2012

City went into the game against West Brom eight points behind Manchester United with just six matches of the Premier League season left to play, our disastrous run of five points from the previous five games leaving Sir Alex Ferguson's side with a seemingly unassailable lead.

But an emphatic victory, coupled with United's shock loss away at Wigan, saw City close the gap to five points with five games left – one of which was a home game against United. It remained a long shot, but there was hope once again where previously there was none.

This was a title race like few others, with shifts in momentum a regular occurrence. City went ahead after six minutes through Sergio Aguero, and the Etihad then erupted early in the second half when news of Shaun Maloney's 20-yard strike for Wigan filtered through.

A quickfire three goals in 10 minutes completed a comprehensive win for City. Aguero scored his second on 54 minutes, before Carlos Tevez, starting his first game since September, and David Silva joined in the goalscoring.

All eyes were then fixed on the DW Stadium. City fans gathered on the concourse at the Etihad to watch (and hope for) the right result to come in. Incredibly, it did. United had failed to score for the first time in 18 matches and Wigan, who had lost all their previous 14 against the Old Trafford side, were out of the relegation zone

thanks to a 1-0 win. It was United's first league defeat in 13 games.

"Wigan were the better team, we were second to every ball and we had one shot on goal," Ferguson admitted afterwards. "It's one of those off nights you get sometimes. We're on a great run that has put us in a position where we can win the league and we just have to get over the disappointment of tonight."

City's defeat to Arsenal three days earlier – a rotten game that had seen Mario Balotelli sent off and an angry post-match interview with manager Roberto Mancini – had surely spelled the end. No one thought City still had a chance, but three days later the title complexion had altered once again.

Mancini, though, was saying otherwise. Whether he meant it or whether it was mind games, we will never know, but he remained steadfast in his belief the title race was over.

"It's finished," Mancini insisted afterwards. "It's finished because United is a fantastic team with fantastic spirit. I think five points is too much.

"For us, it is important to finish well our season – this is our best season in the last 50 years. I am very proud of the players and what they have done until now.

"Maybe we did some mistakes in the last games but it's important to do a good performance."

It remained a difficult task but the latest momentum shift was perhaps enough to unsettle United.

Norwich City 1-6 City

TEVEZ SCORES HAT-TRICK IN SCINTILLATING CARROW ROAD DISPLAY

14 April 2012

City travelled to Norwich on the back of a sizeable swing in the title race three days earlier. Our win against West Brom combined with United's shock 1-0 defeat at Wigan meant we were five points behind our rivals with five league games remaining.

Most experts still felt it unlikely we would overhaul United and win the Premier League title, but one thing was for certain: anything less than a win at Carrow Road would surely hammer the final nail in our coffin.

What ensued was one of City's most free-flowing and ruthless displays of the season as we hit Norwich for six and reduced United's lead at the top to just two points, putting pressure on the leaders going into their game in hand at home to Aston Villa the following day.

Carlos Tevez scored a brilliant hat-trick – his third treble in City colours – and Sergio Aguero scored two, including one of the best goals in our history, a thunderous half-volley from Tevez's instinctive back-heel, as we won 6-1.

Tevez's first was an absolute screamer that swerved into the near top corner from 25 yards after David Silva had stolen possession in midfield and played a one-two with Aguero.

Our second was even better. Tevez played an ingenious first-time backheel to Aguero, who volleyed home powerfully from the edge of the area for one of the goals of this or any other season.

Norwich halved the deficit six minutes into the second half when Andrew Surman finished after a poor punch from Joe Hart, but City found an extra gear thereafter. Tevez headed home after John Ruddy spilled Yaya Touré's shot to make it 3-1, before Aguero produced a wonderful solo effort to make it four.

Tevez pounced on a sloppy backpass to round Ruddy for his hat-trick, which he celebrated with the now famous 'golf swing' celebration, a message, perhaps, to those who had questioned his desire during his unauthorised leave of absence.

But none of that mattered now; this was a vintage City display, rounded off by Adam Johnson's strike in added time, full of quick passing and attacking intent. City were brilliant from start to finish, and Aguero almost made it two City hat-tricks in one day, but for his late effort to hit the post.

"I am happy because we did a fantastic performance," manager Roberto Mancini asserted afterwards. "I am very pleased with my players.

"Tevez has improved a lot in the last weeks and for this reason he played against West Bromwich. I was so worried because he played 48 hours ago, but Carlos is strange. He can play two games in two days and score.

"I am happy for the fans because we are here for them."

Indeed, the City fans made the long journey home from East Anglia delighted with what they had witnessed. They had been desperate to see Tevez and Aguero start together regularly, but Tevez's five-month absence from the side after his refusal to come on as a substitute in a Champions League tie away at Bayern Munich had denied them the opportunity.

Aguero had been deployed alongside Edin Dzeko or Mario Balotelli for much of the season, but this performance against Norwich confirmed what the City fans had long suspected: that Tevez and Aguero, given the chance to flourish, would represent the best strike pairing in the Premier League.

This was the first time since November City had scored more than once away from home in the Premier League and our first league win on the road since 12 February. It was a well-timed victory and the kind of performance that can lift an entire club.

The following day saw United beat Aston Villa to re-established a five-point lead over City at the top of the Premier League table.

But City's victory at Carrow Road had reenergised them. With four games left to play, United had a five-point advantage. They were still favourites, but City now looked back to their best, should there be any more slip-ups from United.

City 1-0 Manchester United
KOMPANY HEADER DECIDES CRUCIAL TITLE SHOWDOWN
30 April 2012

It was one of the most nerve-wracking evenings the Etihad has ever seen. The equation was simple: beat Manchester United and City's first league title in 44 years was ours to lose with just two winnable matches of the season remaining.

Of course, the task was anything but simple. United were our great rivals and English football's dominant side over the previous two decades, and this was the biggest Manchester derby in recent memory, with the media hype in the lead up to the game unlike anything City had ever experienced.

The tension inside the stadium was palpable, both in the stands and on the pitch.

United came into the game in poor form, having dropped five points in their previous three matches. With City winning three on the bounce, recovering well after a serious wobble that had seen us take two points from nine, the momentum was with Roberto Mancini's side.

The previous Matchday had been pivotal. United had drawn 4-4 at home to Everton in the early kick off, with the Merseysiders coming from 4-2 down to take a point. It was Steven Pienaar who scored the late equaliser that blew the title race wide open, before revealing a 'God is Great' t-shirt as he ran away in celebration. It's now ingrained as an iconic Manchester City image.

A few hours later, City went to Wolves and did the business in thoroughly professional fashion, winning 2-0 at Molineux to close the gap on United to three points. Crucially, City also boasted a vastly superior goal difference.

Win this Manchester derby and it would mean the title was ours to lose with just two games of the season remaining.

"I don't think I'd ever gone into a derby thinking that we were going to win but, secretly, this time I did," says Andrew Green, a season ticket holder since 1995. "I think this was brought on by the fear in some United fans I know - I don't think I'd ever known that before. They were fearing the worst."

Sir Alex Ferguson's team selection was unusually cautious, with Wayne Rooney on his own upfront, ahead of a five-man midfield. United, it seemed, were playing for the point that would leave them in control of the title race.

City were the more adventurous side and deservedly took the lead just before half-time, Vincent Kompany climbing higher than Chris Smalling and powering home a header from David Silva's corner. The Belgian's celebration said it all: an outpouring of emotion that has subsequently become one of the defining images of our history.

"It's like [Sergio] Aguero, those

kind of players make it happen in the big games," Micah Richards says of Kompany delivering when City needed him the most.

"It's not a fluke," Joleon Lescott adds. "The big players don't score the big goals by luck."

"The goal is one of those you dream about," Green says. "The celebration stands out as one of the most joyous moments of pure relief and happiness in my life. I've been obsessed with Manchester City for as long as I could walk and talk - that goal and that celebration and that player and that team embody everything I wanted Manchester City to be. It was bliss."

The second-half remained a cagey, tactical affair. United brought on another striker, with Danny Welbeck replacing Park Ji-Sung, but it failed to spark them into life. Carlos Tevez made way for Nigel De Jong with around 20 minutes remaining, and Micah Richards came on for David

Silva as Mancini looked to see the game out.

In truth, City were comfortable, and even had chances in the closing stages to extend our lead, and when the final whistle blew the outpouring of relief from the stands was like nothing we had experienced at the Etihad before.

"The game itself is a blur to me," Green adds. "My memory is that of a United team clearly playing for the solitary point that would suffice but it totally working against them. They showed us that the FA Cup semi-final [in 2011} and the 6-1 [earlier in this season] had frightened them more than we had imagined. They were scared, Ferguson was scared...they were playing for a draw."

The result meant victory in our last two games, away at Newcastle United and at home to Queens Park Rangers, would seal our first title since 1967-68.

"We are happy, but it don't change nothing," Mancini said afterwards,

striking a typically cautionary note. "We have two really difficult games. United will play two easy games. I think United have a slight advantage."

Three weeks before this game, City were eight points adrift of United. Now, with two left to play, we were ahead on goal difference, with an eight-goal advantage. The shift had been remarkable.

"They defend with all players for the whole game," Mancini added. "Also in the second half, they pushed more but didn't have any chances to score. We did a good performance; we knew before it'd be a difficult game because United are a top team.

"I'm very happy for Vincent because he deserved the goal."

Ferguson was magnanimous in defeat and accepted his side didn't deserve anything from the game. "We didn't test the goalkeeper enough," he said. "The longer the half went on, we were looking for half time. And losing a goal at that time is a bad time.

"After that, they played on the counter-attack. I can't complain about the result – they were more of a threat from counter-attacks and we didn't really test the goalkeeper.

"They're in the driving seat. They only need to win two games of football, so we're up against it."

The City fans left the Etihad in a frazzled state, nerves shredded after a tense, almost unbearable, 90-minute experience.

Surely now, with our hardest assignment out of the way, it would be a straightforward sprint for the finish line?

Newcastle United 0-2 City

YAYA DOUBLE PUTS CITY ON THE BRINK OF TITLE SUCCESS

6 May 2012

Yaya Touré had proven he was the man for the big occasion 12 months before this game when he bagged winning goals in both the semi-final and final of the FA Cup, bringing to an end our 35-year wait for silverware.

But he enhanced his credentials even further with a brace against Newcastle at St James' Park to put City one win away from a first league title in 44 years. In times of extreme need, Yaya was the man who would step up and deliver.

His first goal came after 70 minutes, a brilliant curling effort that flew past Newcastle goalkeeper Tim Krul, before the Ivorian sealed the win by finishing off a swift counter with a minute remaining.

Cue delirium in the away section high above the pitch.

"It was a foretaste of the utter dominance Yaya Touré would come to exert in the 2013-14 season," Jonathan Derbyshire, a City fan since the 1970s, says. "It's often forgotten what a difficult game this was – Newcastle were going for a Champions League place and had won away at Chelsea.

"I remember travelling to the game with friends and none of us were particularly confident, but it was a performance of extraordinary control, and I don't ever remember a great

deal of jeopardy in the game. But Yaya didn't score his first until late on, so the tension was excruciating.

"It was one of the most enjoyable journeys back from a City game I think I've ever had."

"Touré's first goal was special, like the one he scored in the FA Cup final for us last year," manager Roberto Mancini said. "This one may be more important if we can finish the season off."

City's match-winning period was sparked by a brilliant substitution from Mancini. On the face of it, replacing Samir Nasri with Nigel De Jong looks like a defensive-minded switch, but with Touré then able to play much higher up the pitch, it allowed him the freedom to damage Newcastle. It was a simple yet wonderfully effective tactical adjustment that won City the game.

"You have to say Manchester City were brilliant today," Newcastle boss Alan Pardew said afterwards. "When you can bring on one world star for another... that freshness just made the difference today. But it is never over in the race for the Premier League title, no matter who your opponents are."

This was a fine win. Newcastle had enjoyed an excellent season and were fifth in the table, with a team containing the likes of Yohan Cabaye, Demba Ba, Papiss Cisse and Hatem Ben Arfa.

But City enjoyed the majority of possession and created the best chances – an exceptional, controlled performance against a very good Newcastle side.

A huge hurdle had been cleared. Surely now, with only a home game against relegation-threatened QPR to come, we were almost home and hosed?

For one final time that season, Mancini had the opportunity to give a cautionary post-match interview. "It is not finished," he stressed. "It is important that we get three points next week, we need a big effort – there is one game more. I think for us it should be a normal week.

"We don't change nothing, QPR will be tough, they are fighting for relegation. Nothing changes. It is ours to lose. It doesn't depend on other teams anymore."

Mike Summerbee was amongst those in the crowd. City's Club Ambassador had played in a 4-3 victory at Newcastle on the final day of the 1967-68 season as

we won the First Division title in spectacular fashion. That was City's last league title success.

The job wasn't done this time around, but City were now tantalisingly close. Summerbee, understandably, had tears in his eyes at the full-time whistle, a roller-coaster season and an emotional 90 minutes taking their toll.

One more game to go...

City 3-2 Queens Park Rangers

ICONIC AGUERO STRIKE EARNS CITY FIRST LEAGUE TITLE IN 44 YEARS

13 May 2012

When the full-time whistle blew at the Etihad Stadium on the final day of the 2011-12 season, there were scenes difficult to describe.

Pandemonium, probably best sums it up.

Manchester City were champions of England for the first time since 1968. There were fans who had seen that triumph, engineered by club greats such as Francis Lee, Colin Bell and Mike Summerbee. There were others who never thought they would witness such an occasion after so much mismanagement, abject failure and spectacular mishaps in the intervening years had left them weary and cynical.

But this was our time.

It wasn't just the outcome that saw bedlam ensue, however. The drama of that special day, which will never fade, made our achievement all the sweeter.

If City were ever going to win the title, doing so in thrilling fashion felt likely – but no one could ever have predicted this. What happened defied belief. Hollywood executives would have rejected this storyline for being too outlandish, too fanciful. "You cannot think of a final game like this," manager Roberto Mancini admitted afterwards. "That would be impossible."

To become champions we only had to win one more game, at home to QPR, managed by former City manager Mark Hughes and threatened with the possibility of relegation. Victory would render second-placed Manchester United's result at Sunderland irrelevant, given our superior goal difference.

And when Pablo Zabaleta scored after 39 minutes, it should have been a straightforward affair, with a carnival atmosphere as the backdrop. Instead, City played miserably thereafter, the magnitude of the occasion denying us our usual fluidity. Nerves had taken control.

Three minutes into the second half, it all started to go badly wrong. Joleon Lescott mistimed a header, Djibril Cisse raced clear and blasted past Joe Hart to make it 1-1. A draw wasn't good enough; United were leading 1-0 at Sunderland thanks to a Wayne Rooney strike and, as it stood, they would be champions.

Former City midfielder Joey Barton was sent off after 55 minutes and all hell broke loose. Sergio Aguero was taken down in the melee, and Barton went after Mario Balotelli on the subs bench. Eventually, referee Mike Dean restored order and the game continued.

Things went from bad to disastrous for City on 66 minutes when Jamie Mackie headed home from Armand Traore's cross to give ten-man QPR the lead.

We were on the brink of a defeat that would have been impossible to live down, the weight of which may have been too difficult to bear. Of all the bad days we had endured, this would top them all – failure on an epic level.

But a miraculous, final few minutes saw us come back from 2-1 down going into stoppage time to win 3-2, at a stroke burying years of pain, heartache and, at times, embarrassment.

Edin Dzeko's header made it 2-2 in the 92nd minute, which at the time felt like a sick joke, the goal that made City's failure even more difficult to bear. What's the closest we could come to winning it but still manage to throw it away?

140 miles north, the Manchester United players and management were celebrating on the pitch at the Stadium of Light having beaten Sunderland and with news of our struggles filtering through.

But then it happened, the Premier League's most iconic moment, 93 minutes and 20 seconds into the game. Aguero picked up a pass from Balotelli, took one touch to steady himself before burying the ball past Paddy Kenny in the QPR goal. Outrageous.

The celebrations were wild, both on the pitch and in the stands. Aguero's shirt came off, Joe Hart ran screaming around his box, Mancini and his team embraced manically, and the fans were throwing themselves in all sorts of directions.

Aguero was immediately immortalised – his place in the pantheon of Premier League greats instantly assured.

For City fans of a certain age, ridicule from our United counterparts for consistent underachievement had been woven into our existence. Now, we had snatched the title from their hands in dramatic style, delivering the most iconic moment in Premier League history in doing so.

"You want to say it's the best moment of my life but if I'm honest please never again this way, please never again!" skipper Vincent Kompany said afterwards in typically eloquent fashion.

"For some reason we've

done it before this season and I've never stopped believing, never ever did I stop believing. When Edin scored that goal, it just reminded me of a few moments this season. Against Tottenham we scored in the last minute, against Sunderland we came back from two goals down.

"We've dreamed of this all of our lives, since we were kids and had nothing. And now we're champions and that's all it's about for us."

Mancini's father, Aldo, who was inside the Etihad that day, had suffered a heart attack two years earlier. Mancini said afterwards he had worried for his father's health, given the dramatic scenes that unfolded.

Chelsea 1-2 City

MANCINI'S MEN MOVE THROUGH TO SECOND FA CUP FINAL IN THREE YEARS

14 April 2013

Manchester City made it through to the FA Cup final for the second time in three years during Roberto Mancini's reign after an absorbing semi-final contest saw us beat Chelsea 2-1 at Wembley.

It capped a fine week, coming just six days after our 2-1 derby win over Manchester United at Old Trafford.

City were by far the better side for the first hour of the encounter and looked to be cruising towards a comfortable victory thanks to goals either side of half-time from Samir Nasri and Sergio Aguero.

Chelsea struggled to cope with Yaya Touré's surging runs all afternoon, and when he put the afterburners on after 34 minutes, it caused panic in their back four.

The Ivorian burst forward and found Aguero inside the box, who slipped a first-time pass to Nasri – and when the Frenchman's attempted return rebounded back at his feet, Nasri swept the ball past Petr Cech from eight yards for his first goal in 20 matches.

Vincent Kompany missed a glorious chance to add to the lead just before the break, skewing the ball wide after Cech had parried James Milner's shot.

Aguero's header early in the second half deservedly doubled our advantage after hitting the post and going in. At that stage, City were very much on top and creating the better chances.

But Chelsea manager Rafa Benitez's tactical switch, which saw him bring on Fernando Torres in place on John Obi Mikel, prompted a revival from the Londoners.

It proved to be a frantic final 30 minutes, which saw City clinging on. Demba Ba scored a fantastic acrobatic goal after 66 minutes; Costel Pantilimon, once again deputising in goal for Joe Hart in a cup competition, made two fine saves; and Chelsea had a decent penalty shout waved away by referee Chris Foy.

The game was a somewhat bad-tempered affair. Aguero was involved in a flashpoint flare-up with David Luiz, and there were a number of fouls in the closing stages.

But in a show of strength and character, City hung on to book another trip to Wembley in May for the final where Wigan Athletic lay in wait.

"I don't think it was one of our better performances of the season," Mancini said afterwards. "After our second goal, we played like it was finished. When they scored, it changed the game.

"We deserved to win this game but nothing is decided.

"In 90 minutes, anything can happen. Wigan play good football and if we want to beat them and win the FA Cup we will have to play a very good game and prepare well."

Given City had beaten a true heavyweight of English football in this hard-fought semi-final encounter, many felt the final, against a Wigan side facing what would be an ultimately doomed battle to avoid relegation, was a fait accompli.

But football often springs surprises.

CITY FOOTBALL GROUP

City have become a byword for innovation during the last decade, and nowhere is our originality more striking than in the creation of the City Football Group (CFG).

Established in May 2013, CFG is the world's leading private owner and operator of football clubs, with total or partial ownership of ten clubs in major cities across the world.

As it stands today, the group comprises Manchester City men's and women's teams in England, New York City FC in the US, Melbourne City men's and women's teams in Australia, Yokohama F. Marinos in Japan, Montevideo City Torque in Uruguay, Girona Futbol Club in Spain, Sichuan Jiuniu FC in China, Mumbai City FC in India, Lommel SK in Belgium, ESTAC in France and Club Bolivar in Bolivia.

And there have been plenty of notable successes since CFG was formed eight years ago, both on and off the pitch.

New York City FC (NYCFC), the first and only Major League Soccer (MLS) team to play in the five boroughs of New York City, have cemented their status as a cornerstone in the landscape of one of the world's most competitive and proudest sporting cities.

NYCFC came into existence as Major League Soccer's 20th franchise on May 21, 2013 and debuted against Orlando City SC in March 2015.

New Yorkers embraced their new club from the start, attracting 20,000 season ticket holders in their inaugural season, as well as drawing an average attendance of 29,000 in their first year, making NYCFC one of the most well-supported teams in the league.

CFG TIMELINE 2013-2015

21 May 2013

Manchester City announce, in partnership with the New York Yankees, the acquisition of the Major League Soccer's 20th expansion club, to be known as New York City Football Club.

22 Jan 2014

City Football Group announced the acquisition of Melbourne Heart Football Club in partnership with the owners of Melbourne Storm.

5 Jun 2014

Melbourne Heart Football Club becomes Melbourne City Football Club.

16 Oct 2014

Manchester City Women lift the Continental Cup in their first season, defeating Arsenal Ladies 1-0 in the final at Wycombe's Adams Park.

20 Nov 2014

Cityzens Giving is launched, giving Cityzens members the opportunity to choose how charity projects around the world are funded.

8 Dec 2014

City Football Academy, Manchester, is officially opened. The 80-acre world-leading youth development and first team facility is now home to Manchester City men's, women's and youth teams, and is the HQ of City Football Group.

27 Feb 2015

City Football Academy, Melbourne, is officially opened. The new facility is the training and administrative hub for Melbourne City FC, and the Asia-Pacific base for City Football Group.

13 Mar 2015

New York City Football Club play their inaugural home game against New England Revolution at Yankee Stadium, defeating the visitors 2-0.

CFG TIMELINE 2016-2017

31 Jan 2016

Melbourne City Women win the 2016 Grand Final after an unbeaten inaugural season.

25 Sep 2016

Manchester City Women beat Chelsea 2-0 to win the WSL title for the first time, following an unbeaten season.

5 Oct 2016

New York City FC announce a permanent training facility in Orangeburg, City Football Academy, New York.

30 Nov 2016

Melbourne City win the FFA Cup final against Sydney FC.

In 2018, NYCFC made the MLS Cup playoffs for the first time after finishing third in the Eastern Conference. The following year, in 2019, NYCFC finished first in the Eastern Conference and reached the MLS Cup playoffs for the second consecutive season.

Sporting Director Dave Lee and Head Coach Ronny Delia, the latter a three-time winning manager at multiple European Clubs including Celtic FC in Scotland, have continued a legacy of beautiful football, building a roster that boasts MLS and international veterans, as well as some of the United States' finest rising stars. In February 2020, they were joined by Nick Cushing, who was named assistant coach following a hugely successful six seasons in charge of Manchester City Women's Football Club, where he led the side to multiple titles.

Their work has proven outstanding. In December 2021, NYCFC secured the ultimate prize in US soccer, winning the MLS Cup with victory over Portland in the final. Off the field, NYCFC have established a world-class academy facility. Opened in 2018 and based in Orangeburg, the New York City FC Academy has a goal of identifying, developing and producing the best local youth soccer players in the New York Metropolitan area. The Club's programme offers a professional and competitive pathway to the highest levels of the game for boys and girls.

The Boys' Academy has seen unprecedented success across domestic competition, winning back-to-back U-19 USSDA National Championships in 2018 and 2019, becoming the first Club to ever do so at that age group. NYCFC's First Team also featured four Homegrown players, including Joe Scally who was sold to German Club Borussia Monchengladbach last year in a move that featured the highest initial transfer fee paid for a 16-year-old MLS player in league history.

12 Feb 2017

Melbourne City Women FC win the W-League.

5 Apr 2017

City Football Group announce the acquisition of Club Atletico Torque, a club based in Montevideo, Uruguay.

13 May 2017

Manchester City Women lift the FA Cup at Wembley, beating Birmingham City Ladies 4-1.

23 Aug 2017

City Football Group acquire 44.3% of Girona FC, who had just won promotion to La Liga.

And NYCFC's contribution to the game goes beyond its own walls. 50 mini-pitches have been created and maintained across the five boroughs of New York thanks to fine work by the New York City Soccer Initiative (NYCSI), which is made up of NYCFC, the Mayor's Fund to Advance New York City, the U.S. Soccer Foundation, Adidas and Etihad Airways.

Melbourne City FC plays its home games at the 30,000 capacity AAMI Park stadium in Melbourne, where the Club celebrated its first ever men's silverware, the FFA Cup, in November 2016.

The Club's training and administrative base is at one of Australia's leading club facilities, City Football Academy, Melbourne, on the campus of La Trobe University.

It features advanced new training pitches for the Melbourne City first team, two elite women's and youth team pitches, dedicated community pitches, world class medical and sports science facilities and expansive office space. It is also CFG's centre for football operations in the Asia Pacific region and the training and administration base for Melbourne City Women's FC, the affiliated Women's team, which was founded in 2015 and competes in the W-League, the top division of women's football in Australia.

In Melbourne City's inaugural season, the women's team completed the season with a 100 per cent record, winning 12 consecutive league matches and clinching the Premier's Plate and securing a historic double, winning the 2016 Grand Final.

In 2017, Melbourne City women's team made history again when they won the Grand Final for a second consecutive year; becoming the first team in the competition to win back-to-back titles. In 2018, the team went one further, entering the realms of sporting elite in completing a fairy-tale three-peat under the direction of former captain, Patrick Kisnorbo.

CFG TIMELINE 2017-2020

9 Nov 2017

Manchester City announce that Amazon will be filming a season-long, access all areas documentary titled All or Nothing: Manchester City.

18 Nov 2017

Club Atletico Torque win promotion to the First Division, becoming the youngest team in the history of the Uruguayan Federation to achieve this feat.

24 Apr 2018

New York City FC unveil their brand new City Football Academy training facility.

20 Feb 2019

CFG purchase Sichuan Jiuniu as part of a consortium including China Sports Capital.

6 Oct 2019

New York City qualify for the CONCACAF Champions League for the first time in their history, having finished top of the MLS Eastern Conference.

28 Nov 2019

City Football Group announce intention to acquire majority stake in Indian Super League side Mumbai City FC. They become the eighth team in the Group.

07 Dec 2019

Yokohama F Marinos win the Japanese J-League for the fourth time in their history, the first time since 2004.

11 May 2020

City football Group acquire Belgian second division side Lommel SK. They become the ninth club in the Group.

In 2020, Melbourne City women's team re-wrote the record books under Head Coach Rado Vidosic, becoming the first team in the competition's history to win four Championship titles after they secured their second invincible season, achieving the Premiership and Championship double after defeating Sydney FC 1-0 at AAMI Park in the 2019-20 Grand Final.

Girona won promotion to La Liga for the first time in its history in May 2017, having reached the playoffs three times in the previous four seasons.

In November 2019, City Football Group agreed a deal to acquire a majority stake in Mumbai City FC in the Indian Super League (ISL), marking a major move into Indian football.

In December 2019, Yokohama were crowned J-League Champions for the fourth time in their history, and the first time since 2004, finishing six points clear of nearest rivals Tokyo FC.

In 2021 Mumbai City FC were crowned Champions of the Hero Indian Super League after a 2-1 win over ATK Mohun Bagan at the Fatorda Stadium in Goa.

Mumbai City FC's victory saw them become the first team in ISL history to secure both the ISL Shield and the ISL Trophy, completing a notable double in the same season.

In 2020-21 ESTAC Troyes finished top of the Ligue 2 securing automatic promotion into Ligue 1.

The creation of CFG was a bold plan, but eight years into the project it's been an undoubted success. The clubs who form the group have access to shared data and a world-wide scouting network, with pathways for players, managers and coaches. There's a mutual understanding of how the game should be played, with the possession-based, attacking football employed most vividly by Manchester City replicated across first-team and academy setups across CFG.

There's more work to be done, but the last eight years has seen hard work, innovation and unequivocal success.

CFG TIMELINE 2020-2021

03 Sep 2020

City Football Group announced that Esperance Sportive Troyes Aube Champagne (ESTAC), in France's Ligue 2, became its tenth club.

12 Jan 2021

Club Bolivar joins City Football Group as first Partner Club.

2021

Four CFG clubs win their respective leagues: Manchester City secure another Premier League title, Mumbai City win the Indian Super League, New York City win MLS Cup and Melbourne City win the A-League. 2021 also sees Troyes promoted.

FERNANDINHO

Widely regarded as one of City's best signings, Fernandinho is loved and admired by both teammates and fans.

He joined in the summer of 2013, having played at Shakhtar Donetsk for six years, and his impact was immediate. He played 46 times in his debut season, with his energetic displays in midfield helping Manuel Pellegrini's side claim a Premier League and League Cup double for the first time in the club's history. Alongside Yaya Touré, he formed part of the most dynamic midfield in English football.

He scored in the 2016 League Cup final and started all 12 matches en route to our Champions League semi-final against Real Madrid. By this stage, he was a firm fan favourite, his reputation as one of the most reliable players in the club's history very much cemented.

Pep Guardiola's arrival in 2016 meant a change in style – but it was immediately clear Fernandinho would be a key part of his plans. "I think Fernandinho can play in 10 positions," he said a month after taking charge. "He has the quality to play wherever. He's a quick, fast player, so intelligent, aggressive and strong in the air." Guardiola values versatility, hard work and professionalism, so it was no surprise the Brazilian had impressed him so soon.

Despite his ability to play in multiple positions, he has been used almost exclusively as a defensive midfielder, and under Guardiola's guidance he has established himself as one of the best in the world. He offers protection to our backline but has the energy and range of passing needed to start attacks from deep – the full modern-day defensive-midfield package.

He played 48 games during our Centurions season and was named in the PFA Team of the Year as City became the first men's team in English football history to win all four domestic trophies in 2018-19, with his potent blend of outstanding technical ability, deep tactical understanding and a tireless work rate vital to our success.

And when David Silva decided to leave City in the summer of 2020, Fernandinho was voted as the new club captain by the players and staff, a deserved honour for a man who has played with distinction throughout his time here, always leading by example on and off the pitch.

"He is an authentic leader and always he is there," Guardiola said of Fernandinho in 2021. "I am so satisfied he was chosen as captain – he represents this club magnificently."

2020-21 was a testing season, with COVID-19 causing a truncated season and relentless fixture calendar. But City won the Premier League and League Cup – and reached the Champions League final for the first time. After a difficult start, a team meeting called and chaired by Fernandinho proved pivotal.

"I really cannot express how important Fernandinho is to us as a group," says Ilkay Gundogan. "He is immense. Obviously, he didn't get as much game time as others in the squad this season but he knows his role, his responsibility, and what he has to say at the right times, as well. This is what a leader is."

He signed a new deal in the summer of 2021, extending his stay at the Etihad Stadium into a ninth season. So far, he has made 350 appearances, winning 12 trophies, including four Premier Leagues and a record six League Cups.

"All the good things that happen to him he deserves, all the uncomfortable jobs for the team, he did it," Pep says.

Ferna arrived at City as a relative unknown. He will leave a bona fide club legend.

MANUEL PELLEGRINI

Manuel Pellegrini succeeded Roberto Mancini in the summer of 2013 and quickly set about altering City's playing style.

The club's owners wanted to evolve. Where Mancini had been somewhat pragmatic and conservative, Pellegrini was charged with releasing the handbrake and ushering in a more fluent, attacking style.

The Chilean's first season in charge was a success as he secured the club's first ever league and cup double, with City scoring a remarkable 156 goals in all competitions.

The signing of Fernandinho was key, the Brazilian's stellar defensive ability and tireless running allowing Yaya Touré greater freedom. With the shackles off, Touré delivered perhaps the greatest season by a central midfielder in recent history, leading City to a first League Cup triumph since 1976 and another Premier League title.

City started well in the league, beating Newcastle and Manchester United easily at the Etihad, but it was a 12-game unbeaten run between the end of November and the end of January that saw us hit new heights. We won 11, including a 6-0 destruction of Tottenham at the Etihad, a 6-3 win over Arsenal, a 2-1 victory over Liverpool and an impressive 5-1 success at White Hart Lane.

We also beat Sunderland 3-1 in an entertaining League Cup final and then won our final five Premier League games of the season, including a 2-0 win at home to West Ham, to seal our second title in three seasons as we finished two points ahead of Liverpool, whose late-season slip had allowed City back in.

Domestically, our only disappointment was a shock home defeat to Wigan Athletic in the FA Cup quarter-final. Pellegrini knows he could – and probably should – have been the first manager to win an English domestic treble. Pellegrini also oversaw our first ever qualification from the Champions League group stage, before succumbing to Barcelona in the last-16.

It was an excellent season for which Pellegrini failed to get the credit he deserved. "Big teams cannot be satisfied with one title," Pellegrini said after sealing the Premier League. "This club and players deserve more titles."

However, the Pellegrini era failed to kick on in the way we had hoped. We started the next season in similar fashion and sat three points off top spot at the halfway point – but a poor second half of the season saw us finish as runners up, eight points behind champions Chelsea. We bagged a league high tally of 83 goals, but that was considerably less than the 102 we managed in the previous campaign.

And the final season saw clear regression. City lost 10 league matches for the first time since 2008/09, managing just 65 points and finishing a disappointing fourth.

We did, however, win another League Cup – beating Liverpool in the final – and made it to our first ever Champions League semi-final, significant progress for a side who'd been capped at the last-16 stage prior to that. Our performance over the two legs in the semi-final against Real Madrid was insipid, though, with the final stages of the game in the Bernabeu, with a solitary goal needed to progress to the final, strangely conservative.

An unforgettable first season, a more fluent style of football and significant improvement in the Champions League. This Charming Man's tenure wasn't perfect, but there were some wonderful highs and City were now ready to take the next step in our development.

MANUEL PELLEGRINI
Managerial statistics

Games	167
Won	100
Drawn	28
Lost	39
Goals For	373
Goals against	180
Goals difference	193
Win Percentage %	59.9%
Trophies	3
Games per trophy	55.7
Start date	14/06/2013
End Date	30/06/2016
Total days	1112

City 4-1 Manchester United

PELLEGRINI LAYS DOWN A MARKER IN FIRST DERBY

22 September 2013

The Manchester football landscape changed drastically in the summer of 2013.

Sir Alex Ferguson had left Manchester United after 26 years in charge. His final season had seen United win the Premier League title for the 13th time under his stewardship. He had then personally selected David Moyes to take over and lead the Old Trafford side into a new era.

Meanwhile Roberto Mancini, the man who had led City to a first league title in 44 years in 2012, had been replaced by Manuel Pellegrini, formerly of Malaga and Real Madrid.

It was a derby to mark the dawn of a new age in Manchester.

It ended in a crushing win for City, with Pellegrini's cavalier side turning on the style to win 4-1, sending out a statement to the rest of the Premier League.

The score was certainly impressive, but it was the manner of the performance that pleased City fans most. The champions were destroyed; City were quicker, sharper, more inventive and ruthless. It was a complete display.

City were rampant from the off and took the lead on 15 minutes. Samir Nasri bamboozled Chris Smalling before slipping in the overlapping Aleks Kolarov. His pinpoint cross was met by Sergio Aguero, who volleyed home first time past David De Gea in emphatic fashion.

Our lead was doubled just before half-time, when Nasri's corner was headed down by Alvaro Negredo for Yaya Touré to finish from close range.

Two goals within five minutes of the restart ended any hopes of a potential United comeback. Aguero bagged another first-time finish after fine work from Negredo and the outstanding Nasri, enjoying one of his best performances in a City shirt, deservedly got on the scoresheet when he volleyed home from Jesus Navas' cross.

Rio Ferdinand and Nemanja Vidic, one of the all-time great Premier League centre-back pairings, were given a torrid time by Aguero, while Touré dictated the midfield battle. Moyes looked shellshocked on the United bench.

It was total domination, with United outclassed in every department. A late Wayne Rooney free-kick – his 11th Manchester derby goal, more than any other player in history – provided a scrap of consolation for Moyes, but City's win could hardly have been more unequivocal.

Indeed, this was arguably a better all-round performance than the 6-1 thrashing at Old Trafford two years earlier.

"When you win against Manchester United 4-1, no-one believes it before the game," Pellegrini said afterwards. "But we have the trust to at least try it. From the first minute, we tried to be the team with possession of the ball and to score goals. We played really well.

"For our team, it was a really important game. Our fans now have four months until the next game [against United] to enjoy it."

With Edin Dzeko, James Milner, Stevan Jovetic, Micah Richards and Joleon Lescott all on the bench, was it difficult for Pellegrini to select a side with so much quality at his disposal?

"No, that's not a problem – the problem is when you don't have players!" Pellegrini added with a smile.

City 6-0 Tottenham
VINTAGE CITY HIT SPURS FOR SIX
24 November 2013

Manchester City's Premier League home form going into the game with Tottenham in November 2013 had been perfect.

Five wins from five. Twenty goals scored. Two conceded. No one could live with us at the Etihad, with Newcastle United, Manchester United and Norwich all suffering heavy defeats thus far.

However, away from home we had struggled, losing four matches against Cardiff City, Aston Villa, Chelsea and Sunderland, and drawing one at Stoke. Our record of won one, drawn one, lost four from our first six games on the road was poor.

Indeed, no team had won the title having lost four matches at this stage of a season since 1968. Clearly, City faced an uphill battle if we were to go on and be crowned champions.

However, if there was any internal concern, Manuel Pellegrini was disguising it well.

"I don't believe in statistics in football," said the City manager. "Football has some relation to mathematics, but not always. We win all the games between now and the end, we may win the Premier League."

Back on home soil, it was time for Tottenham to visit the Etihad and to see if they could stem the tide of City goals.

The answer was a resounding no.

Pellegrini's side produced perhaps the finest display of the season so far, winning 6-0 to move up to fourth in the table, six points adrift of leaders Arsenal.

Jesus Navas scored twice – one after 13 seconds that provided the perfect start and one in injury time –

Sandro was unlucky to score an own goal, Sergio Aguero bagged a double and fellow striker Alvaro Negredo continued his fine form with a fifth league goal of the season so far.

Spurs were completely overpowered and overwhelmed, suffering their biggest league defeat since losing 7-1 to Newcastle in December 1996.

City proved superior in every department with the defence looking solid, Yaya Touré and Fernandinho bossing the middle and Aguero, Negredo and Navas at times virtually unplayable.

City's performance was little short of sensational. But once again, observers were left confused as to why we could not replicate that devastating home form on the road.

"We played really well. We are working to have one style of playing and to continue in the same way," Pellegrini said afterwards.

"All my teams normally score a lot of goals. At Real Madrid, we scored more than 100 goals in the whole season. But here we have not only Sergio Aguero and Alvaro Negredo, who are both incredible players, we also have Edin Dzeko and Stevan Jovetic, who is injured.

"You cannot also forget about Fernandinho and Samir Nasri as they played really well against Tottenham.

"In this style the players are comfortable because they are creative players."

Pellegrini's preferred brand of football was one of the main reasons he had been installed as manager during the summer – and this was another shining example of his City squad's capability now the handbrake had been removed and all-out attacking football was being encouraged.

Bayern Munich 2-3 City

CITY HALT BAYERN'S CHAMPIONS LEAGUE WINNING RUN WITH SUPERB VICTORY

10 December 2013

City produced a stunning comeback to beat Bayern Munich 3-2 at the Allianz Arena on a night of bizarre drama in Bavaria.

The German side stormed to a two-goal lead inside 12 minutes, Thomas Muller and Mario Gotze doing the damage. At that stage Bayern appeared to be cruising to an 11th consecutive Champions League win.

But City's level improved drastically, and David Silva cut the arrears after 28 minutes with a close-range finish, before Aleksandr Kolarov's penalty and a James Milner strike put Manuel Pellegrini's side ahead in the second half.

A 3-2 win for City meant a second-placed finish in Group D, level on 15 points with Bayern, but one more goal would mean we top the group. UEFA rules state that when teams finish level on points in the Champions League, group positions are decided by head-to-head records – not goal difference – and given Pep Guardiola's side had won 3-1 at the Etihad, a 4-2 victory on the night in southern Germany would have seen us take top spot.

Confusion reigned. Pellegrini admitted afterwards he wasn't aware of the rules, with the City manager opting to bring Jack Rodwell off the bench and leaving Sergio Aguero as an unused substitute during the final period when one more goal would have been enough.

Despite that, City almost did score a fourth, when Bayern 'keeper Manuel Neuer saved from Alvaro Negredo at the death.

"After they scored the first goal, I continued [thinking] that 3-1 was not enough because they had a better goal difference, so I continued [to think] that we had to win by three goals, 3-0 or 4-1," Pellegrini revealed.

"That was my mistake, but not many teams score four goals against Bayern Munich.

"I am not afraid of who we are going to play in the round of 16. I believe the 16 best teams in Europe are all exactly the same for us. The trust the team has after beating Bayern Munich in their own stadium, that is much, much more important than being first in the group."

Regardless of the uncertainty, this was a statement win for City in a competition that had provided more downs than ups. We once again showed we could marry steely determination and defensive solidity with attacking brilliance. When City were at their best under Pellegrini, it was a fine sight.

Arsenal, City's opponents at the Etihad in four days' time, would have been interested observers and they were left under no illusions that to get a result against us, they would have to be at their absolute maximum.

City 6-3 Arsenal

RUTHLESS CITY MAINTAIN IMPERIOUS HOME FORM WITH THUMPING WIN

14 December 2013

"All his teams play attractive football, that is what people want to see," Samir Nasri said in the summer of 2013 in reaction to the news Manuel Pellegrini had been appointed City boss. "You pay for tickets to go to football to see something great, and he is the kind of manager who can do it."

Nasri's words had proven prophetic. Since Pellegrini was installed, City had become the Premier League's great entertainers, scoring 41 times in our 15 league matches so far.

At the Etihad, in particular, our ruthless attacking quality was in clear evidence. In our seven home games so far, City had scored a remarkable 29 goals.

Given our fantastic goalscoring record – as well as being on the back of an outstanding Champions League win away against Pep Guardiola's Bayern Munich four days earlier – Arsene Wenger's Arsenal must have arrived in Manchester with a feeling of trepidation. City had already overwhelmed Newcastle, Manchester United and Tottenham – and put seven past Norwich – in the early weeks of the season. It was becoming known we had the capability to tear teams apart, if we hit top gear.

What ensued was an Etihad classic, two attack-minded teams going toe to toe for supremacy, sharing nine goals,

with City once again hitting six. We were not just beating teams at home, we were completely taking them apart.

Sergio Aguero, as so often, got City off the mark after 14 minutes, volleying home superbly at the back post after Martin Demichelis' flick on. Aguero now had 19 goals in all competitions for the season, including 13 in the Premier League – one more than his entire league tally in 2012-13.

The movement of Aguero and strike partner Alvaro Negredo was causing Arsenal all sorts of problems, as was the pace and power of Yaya Touré in midfield, with City creating a plethora of chances in the early stages.

But the visitors equalised when Theo Walcott's first-time finish from the edge of the area beat City 'keeper Costel Pantilimon.

Negredo put the ball wide when clean through, a disappointing end to a wonderfully worked opportunity, but he made amends moments later when he tapped home Pablo Zabaleta's inviting ball across the box. It was a move of pure quality.

City deservedly led at the end of a breathless first 45 minutes.

The second half, however, was arguably even better. Fernandinho curled a brilliant effort from outside the area past Wojciech Szczesny to register his first City goal, but Walcott once again cut the arrears with a fine finish into the top corner just past the hour mark.

But three minutes later, our two-goal lead was restored when David Silva finished from Jesus Navas' low cross, and Fernandinho soon made it 5-2 with a deft chip over Szczesny.

Per Mertesacker reduced the deficit to 5-3 deep into stoppage time, but City still had time for another. Man of the match Fernandinho slipped in James Milner, who rounded Szczesny before being brought down by the Arsenal 'keeper. Touré's penalty ended the scoring.

Arsenal had played their part in a Premier League classic – but City were the superior side.

"Today we scored six goals against the best team in the league as they are top of the Premier League table and have the best defence in the league as they had only conceded 11 goals," Pellegrini said afterwards.

"We scored six and missed at least four or five clear goals more.

"We have a lot more points to fight for; we have to keep improving. For me it is very important to be an entertaining team, but for me it will be more entertaining if we score six and concede none.

"We are still three points behind Arsenal and there are still five or six teams that want to win the league. It will continue to the end, and we must try to win more points.

"I think the game Fernandinho played was perfect. He was incredible and didn't make any mistakes. Not only did he score two goals but the way he recovered balls; I know what a big player he is."

Another thumping win, with 35 Premier League home goals already plundered. If we could find some consistency away from home, we would take some stopping.

City 6-0 West Ham United

ONE FOOT IN THE LEAGUE CUP FINAL AS NEGREDO BAGS HAT-TRICK

8 January 2014

Another scintillating home showing saw City all-but assure a place in the 2014 League Cup final thanks to a 6-0 win over West Ham in the first leg of our semi-final tie.

City were chasing a first final appearance since 1976, when Dennis Tueart's brilliant overhead kick sealed a 2-1 victory over Newcastle United at Wembley, and a devastating display saw us establish a seemingly impregnable lead to take into the Upton Park return.

City were inspired by Spanish striker Alvaro Negredo, with 'The Beast' claiming a magnificent hat-trick to round off another dynamic exhibition of outstanding attacking football as we further enhanced our reputation as the best side in England to watch.

Negredo struck twice inside the opening half hour with Yaya Touré also on target in the first half as Sam Allardyce's side were blown away, the Hammers going in three down at the break amidst driving rain.

Negredo's 18th of the campaign completed his hat-trick shortly after the restart, and Yaya Touré continued his own fine form by scoring the fourth.

Edin Dzeko added further gloss to the scoreline with a brace of his own, finishing off what was a wonderful night for the City fans.

It was the sixth time City had scored five or more in the 2013-14 season. Furthermore, this latest victory meant City had now won 14 of our 15 home games this season, with the only defeat coming in the Champions League against Bayern Munich. Along the way, Pellegrini's side had chalked up 59 goals at the Etihad and conceded just 13.

After the game, Manuel Pellegrini said he was delighted with his players' all-round intensity, with and without the ball.

"It was a brilliant performance. Not only because we scored six goals but also by the way the team played across the 90 minutes," said the City manager.

"It doesn't matter if we are winning 2-0, 3-0... we try to play the same way and to score more goals.

"Today was a very important step to try and play in the final. Alvaro made a great match, not only for the three goals he scored, but he was a link with the midfielders and the strikers we have and also he recovered a lot of balls."

City would go on to win the second leg 3-0, completing a record 9-0 aggregate success – the biggest margin of victory in a League Cup semi-final tie.

It booked our place in a League Cup final for the first time in 38 years. Sunderland, who would overcome Manchester United in the other semi-final, were our opponents.

With City also in contention to win the Premier League title, a league-and-cup double remained a distinct possibility for Pellegrini's cavalier entertainers.

Tottenham 1-5 City

AGUERO TURNS ON THE STYLE IN NORTH LONDON

29 January 2014

When Manchester City clicked during Manuel Pellegrini's first season in charge, it was a thing of great beauty for fans to behold.

The emphatic win away at Tottenham in January 2014, which saw us leapfrog Arsenal and go top of the Premier League table, was one such occasion. It was a showcase blend of strength, pace, power and creativity – an ominous performance that saw us dismantle Spurs in every department.

Tottenham came into the game rejuvenated after the appointment of Tim Sherwood as manager but City soon assumed total control.

For the 45 minutes he was on the pitch before suffering a hamstring injury – the only disappointment on an otherwise wonderful night for City in north London – Sergio Aguero was completely unplayable.

The Argentine striker seemed turbocharged – the Tottenham defenders could not live with him – and he scored a goal after 15 minutes that set City on the way to a fine win. It was a masterclass from Aguero, the kind to which City fans had already become accustomed.

The goal was Aguero's 50th in the Premier League in just his 81st appearance, making him the fifth-fastest player to reach a half century.

The second half saw much the same pattern of play, with City dictating proceedings.

Danny Rose was sent off four minutes after the restart for a tackle on Edin Dzeko. The Spurs left-back did appear to make contact with the ball and a red card and penalty felt harsh. However,

Yaya Touré scored from the spot to double City's lead.

Dzeko made it 3-0 two minutes later as City threatened a repeat of the 6-0 triumph over Tottenham in the reverse fixture in November, a win that sparked a superb run of 11 wins and one draw in 12 league matches.

Etienne Capoue pulled one back for Spurs, before Stevan Jovetic, who had replaced Aguero, scored his first league goal since joining from Fiorentina, with Vincent Kompany's 89th-minute effort completing the victory.

It was yet another demonstration of City's exceptional goalscoring ability. And it was now 40 goals in our last 12 league matches.

"City are the best team on the planet," was Tottenham manager Tim Sherwood's assessment. "Even before the red card it was difficult against this team."

For Pellegrini, City's wonderful form was full justification for his attacking approach.

"I'm delighted not only because we are at the top of the league, but the team played very well," said the City boss. "Away from home maybe that is the best we have played, it is a good moment. It is not easy to score here in this stadium and I repeat we missed at least five or six clear chances.

"We defended well, that's why the performance was complete. They are a very good team who are in a good moment. We missed at least five, but we scored five.

"We are not thinking about the title because we still have 15 games to play, it is important."

It was a night to remember at White Hart Lane.

City 3-1 Sunderland
TOURÉ SCORES WEMBLEY CLASSIC AS CITY LIFT LEAGUE CUP
2 March 2014

City won the League Cup for the first time since 1976 after an inspired second-half performance saw off Sunderland at Wembley in a thoroughly entertaining final.

Manuel Pellegrini's side were deservedly behind at the break after Fabio Borini's goal on 10 minutes but stepped it up significantly in the second half, scoring three times, including two in the space of a minute.

The first 45 minutes saw slow, lacklustre football from City, with Sunderland's aggression and enthusiasm causing us to panic. But the second period saw order restored, with Pellegrini's players finding fluidity and creativity as Sunderland were picked apart.

Not since Dennis Tueart's famous overhead kick at the old Wembley Stadium against Newcastle United 38 years earlier had City won this competition.

That goal has long been considered the finest to grace a League Cup final, but Yaya Touré's equaliser here may well eclipse it.

The Ivorian hit a stupendous first-time effort from 25 yards that flew into the top corner to spark City into life – a mind-bending effort that sent the travelling City fans into a state of exhilaration.

Asked if it was the best goal of his career so far, Touré admitted: "I think so, yes. It was important as well. We needed to win today. The final is only one game and you need to enjoy it – but you need to win."

Seconds later, the noise levels inside Wembley rose even further when Samir Nasri produced a beautiful outside-of-the-foot strike that flew past Black Cats 'keeper Vito Mannone to give us the lead.

And Jesus Navas then sealed the win – and the trophy – with a superb first-time strike in the dying moments of the game to finish off a fine counter-attack from City.

Joleon Lescott was left on the bench for the final, despite playing every minute of the previous rounds, with Pellegrini partnering Martin Demichelis alongside Vincent Kompany at the heart of City's back four. Sergio Aguero came straight back into the side to partner Edin Dzeko, whose League Cup record had seen him score in all four previous rounds.

For Pellegrini, this represented a significant moment in his career. It was the Chilean's first trophy in English football, and the platform, he hoped, for further success.

"I'm very happy," he said. "To win the first trophy I think is important for us all. For the players, for me and for the staff – everyone. It's very important, because at an important club you must win trophies.

"We deserved to win this cup. We scored 22 goals and conceded just two. The first half maybe we were nervous. But we had the maturity, patience and trust to turn the game."

City captain Vincent Kompany was euphoric at the full-time whistle, describing the occasion as "special".

"It's the best stadium. For me it's the best in Europe, maybe even the world, and lifting the trophy here is something special," the skipper insisted.

"We never take anything for granted and we'll enjoy every moment. I think we should be hungry for more. We've achieved something great for the club and now we need to carry on."

Hull City 0-2 City
SILVA MASTERCLASS TURNS TITLE RACE
15 March 2014

There are pivotal matches in every season, those days where momentum shifts and the picture alters dramatically. In 2013/14, that day came in mid-March, with City away at Hull and our title ambitions hanging by a thread.

We went into the game third in the table, behind Liverpool and Chelsea with 12 matches remaining, and bruised by two cup exits in the space of four days. Our previous match, away at Barcelona in the UEFA Champions League, had finished just 63 hours earlier.

A win was vital, but inside ten minutes inspirational captain Vincent Kompany was sent off for a foul on Nikica Jelavic.

The game – and our title hopes – seemed over, but David Silva conjured a mesmeric display full of vision, skill and technical quality; a virtuoso performance that saw his ability to conduct the orchestra cast in full colour.

Hull couldn't live with him. His ability to keep the ball was key given our numerical disadvantage, as was his ability to summon vital contributions.

He scored a beauty four minutes after Kompany's dismissal and produced a fine outside-of-the-boot pass in the build-up to Edin Dzeko's 90th-minute strike to secure a critical 2-0 win. He was withdrawn a minute later, Manuel Pellegrini offering the travelling supporters an opportunity to show their appreciation for what they had just witnessed.

Another star at the KC Stadium was Martin Demichelis, a player who had received strong criticism going into the game having given away a penalty in the shock FA Cup defeat to Wigan the previous weekend. He was superb, marshalling City's high defensive line brilliantly. Without Kompany, City needed a leader and he stepped forward admirably.

"I think he [Demichelis] has played well all season," Pellegrini said afterwards. "Maybe he gave away one penalty against Wigan that was unnecessary, but I haven't agreed with all the criticism he's received.

"It was a very good response for the team. After a difficult week and playing with one man less for most of the game, I think it was a very important performance."

The result sparked City into life after a turbulent couple of weeks. We dropped just seven points from our final 11 matches – a magnificent run that saw us pounce on the title as Liverpool faltered and slipped in the final weeks. That game, unquestionably, was the turning point, and Silva himself looks back on that as one of his favourite matches during his time at City.

Crystal Palace 0-2 City

CITY ASSUME CONTROL ON DAY OF HIGH DRAMA

27 April 2014

Few City fans will ever forget 27 April, 2014. Manuel Pellegrini's side started the day third in the table, six points behind leaders Liverpool, who appeared to be closing in on their first title in 24 years having won 11 league games on the spin.

But in the day's early kick-off, Chelsea, managed by Jose Mourinho, delivered a tactical masterclass at Anfield and left with a shock 2-0 victory, a result that blew the title race wide open.

Chelsea selected a five-man midfield, offering plenty of protection to their back four, in a move that frustrated Liverpool, a side known for their ability to overpower teams in the early stages of games at Anfield. It was classic Mourinho, revelling in his role of party pooper.

Steven Gerrard slipped and failed to control a Mamadou Sakho pass, allowing Demba Ba to race clear and score past Simon Mignolet three minutes into first-half stoppage time.

And in the closing moments, Willian scored on the counter to seal a famous win.

The result ended Liverpool's 16-match unbeaten streak and meant the title was no longer in their control.

All eyes then switched to Selhurst Park. If City could win at Crystal Palace, we would seize the initiative with three games left to play.

The tension in the away section was palpable, but Edin Dzeko soon settled City nerves, heading home from Yaya Touré's inviting cross and celebrating with the away fans. You could almost feel the nerves dissipate, allowing City to play with complete freedom.

Touré had been our best player all season but had missed the previous two matches with a muscle injury. He was back to his unplayable best in south London, and after laying on the first, he then scored our second in typical swashbuckling fashion. He picked the ball up deep in his own half, played a one-two with Dzeko and another with Samir Nasri, before setting off on one of his trademark runs. Damien Delaney tried to halt Yaya's progress on the edge of the area, but Touré simply flicked the ball past him before imperiously curling the ball into the top corner.

Another moment of pure genius from a player operating at the very top of his game.

"It was a happy day," City boss Manuel Pellegrini beamed afterwards. "It was a very important win for us. Before today, we were depending on other teams. Now we continue as we were two weeks ago, depending only on what we do.

"It was important to get a good start but also not to let Crystal Palace score. It was a very professional performance. But it's not finished, we have to play three games more. Anything can happen. Pressure is different for different teams.

"We are not thinking about goal difference. We just concentrate on winning the next game."

City remained in third, but – as Pellegrini alluded – with a crucial game in hand over both Liverpool and second-placed Chelsea as well as a superior goal difference, it meant wins against Everton away and Aston Villa and West Ham United at home, in our final three matches, would seal our second title in three seasons.

This was the day everything swung back in City's favour – the destiny of the title race in our hands once again. We knew we couldn't let it slip now.

Everton 2-3 City

CITY RETURN TO PREMIER LEAGUE SUMMIT AFTER GOODISON CLASSIC

3 May 2014

City fans are used to drama, but experience doesn't make it any easier to bear.
This game away at Everton can be neatly filed in the ever-expanding annals of City's most nerve-shredding matches. It was almost unbearable.

City knew three wins from our final three Premier League games would seal our second title in three seasons. The toughest of those assignments was the trip to Goodison Park, a ground which was home to many painful memories for City fans. One win in our previous 14 visits told its own story.

"It was really, really tense," says Murdoch Dalziel, a lifelong City fan and season ticket holder since 1981. "All the time the game was going on, Everton's record against us at Goodison was in the back of my mind. It's definitely in my top five most stressful games."

City started well and were playing with the kind of intensity you would expect, given what was at stake. Sergio Aguero danced through the Everton defence and slid in Pablo Zabaleta who had come steaming forward from right-back, but he miscued his effort and it went over the bar.

Ross Barkley then scored a spectacular goal after 11 minutes to make City's task that much harder. Some Everton fans didn't know whether to celebrate, given any points taken off City would see Liverpool back in pole position to win their first league title since 1990. It was a remarkable moment of genius from Barkley, who had curled the ball over Joe Hart and into the back of the net from 20 yards with minimal backlift.

But City reasserted control and began to dictate play. Yaya Touré curled one effort over the bar from a decent position before Aguero, who looked so sharp early on, levelled affairs after 22 minutes with a powerful near-post drive that flew past Tim Howard in the Everton goal.

However, the Argentine striker was forced off with a groin injury shortly after, replaced by Fernandinho.

Undeterred, City continued to control the game, and two minutes before half-time we were ahead. Dzeko's shot forced a save from Howard with his feet, but the ball landed at the feet of James Milner. He took a touch to go past Leighton Baines and hung an inviting ball into the box where Dzeko, despite going backwards, planted a wonderful header past Howard.

"Dzeko's header from Milner's cross

– very few players in Premier League history could have scored that goal," Dalziel says. "It was an incredible header."

Within a minute of the second half starting, Hart produced a crucial save. Barkley charged forward fully 60 yards and threaded a superb through-ball into the path of Steven Naismith, who took a touch and curled a shot towards the bottom corner. It was going in, but Hart's outstretched left arm tipped it round the post. Sensational.

Dzeko scored again two minutes later to extend City's lead, turning home Nasri's low cross after the Frenchman had ghosted past John Stones. The away fans let loose, with a collective release of tension and emotion.

But Romelu Lukaku's diving header went in off the post with 25 minutes remaining to set up a nervous finale.

City needed to employ any tactic necessary to ensure we got over the line, and Dzeko, the hero of the day, went down for six minutes towards the end to eat up valuable time.

"Joe Hart's save from Naismith was

key," Dalziel says. "But the star of the show was Dzeko, who went down playing dead for six minutes to run the clock down! We didn't bring on a physio, we knew what we were doing – brilliant game-management from everyone."

City had done it. The final whistle blew and we were now just two wins from the title.

"Zabaleta's celebration in front of the fans at the end – and the outpouring of emotion and release of stress – was just incredible," Dalziel recalls.

"It shows the character of the team – playing away, going behind and we could turn the match," manager Manuel Pellegrini said afterwards.

The equation now was simple: Beat Aston Villa and West Ham United – both at home – and the title would be ours.

City 4-0 Aston Villa

ROUTINE VICTORY AS CITY TIME RUN TO PERFECTION

7 May 2014

Only one more hurdle to clear.

City's thumping 4-0 win over Aston Villa in our penultimate Premier League game of the 2013-14 campaign moved us tantalisingly close to being crowned champions for the second time in three seasons. A victory against West Ham United at the Etihad four days later and the title was ours.

This result was never in doubt, and although the scoreline was perhaps a little unfair on Villa, City thoroughly deserved the three points.

That said, it took City until 64 minutes to go in front, Edin Dzeko finishing from close range after Pablo Zabaleta had crossed along the six-yard box. It was just the latest example of Dzeko's propensity for scoring important goals.

A similar routine brought about City's second. Zabaleta, again marauding down the right, cut the ball back for Samir Nasri, whose shot was saved by Brad Guzan – but Dzeko was there to swallow up the rebound and finish emphatically.

Andreas Weimann hit the crossbar with a header to provide City with a scare, but Stevan Jovetic made it 3-0 with a strike from the edge of the area after Yaya Touré had led three Villa defenders a merry dance.

And it was fitting that Touré scored our fourth, a goal that sparked wild celebrations, given the titanic season the Ivorian had enjoyed. It's doubtful we'll see another central midfielder deliver such consistent brilliance over the course of an entire campaign.

His goal here was archetypal

Yaya – driving from halfway, leaving defenders trailing behind him, before slamming home an unstoppable finish. He now had 24 goals in all competitions, including 20 in the Premier League alone. Staggering numbers that further underlined his quality.

City were top going into the final day and we had got there in style. Touré's goal against Villa was the 100th we had scored in the Premier League – and the 154th in all competitions. This was the 16th occasion under manager Manuel Pellegrini we had scored four or more goals.

This is exactly what City's owners and leadership team had wanted when the Chilean was installed: beautiful, attacking football that brings glittering rewards.

"There are different ways to win titles," Pellegrini pointed out. "I choose this one: attractive football. We have a style of play. We are an attractive team, we score many goals and we are always thinking to score more. That, to me, has the same importance as winning the title."

The Etihad fans were joyous at the full-time whistle, just three weeks after the despondency of the 2-2 draw at home to bottom side Sunderland – a result that appeared to have killed off our title hopes. How crucial that late Samir Nasri equaliser against the Black Cats felt now.

Having spent just 11 days at the top of the table before this game with Villa, City had timed the final sprint to perfection. The Premier League crown was now ours to lose, with just one very winnable home match remaining.

Where had we heard that before?

City 2-0 West Ham

CITY WIN PREMIER LEAGUE FOR SECOND TIME IN THREE YEARS

11 May 2014

Manchester City were crowned champions of England for the second time in three years, finishing two points ahead of Liverpool after a dramatic title race that had seen the pendulum swing back and forth during a frenzied final few months of the season.

Liverpool's defeat to Chelsea and incredible collapse away at Crystal Palace saw their title charge stall, and City won five games in a row to usurp the Merseysiders and end the season as Premier League champions.

But whereas the title triumph of two years earlier involved last-day drama of epic proportions, there were no such difficulties this time. City's title confirmation was relatively serene on this occasion after goals either side of the half-time break from Samir Nasri and Vincent Kompany secured a comfortable 2-0 win over West Ham United in our final game.

As the full-time whistle blew at the Etihad, jubilant supporters poured onto the pitch and wild celebrations began. This new era of success, which had started in 2011 with an FA Cup win, showed no signs of abating and the City fans were enjoying every minute.

Our title success was a fitting reward for City's fine attacking football. We ended the campaign having scored a remarkable 156 goals in all competitions – a new record for a top-flight English side – including 102 in the Premier League alone.

Yaya Touré, who produced a vintage season, was our top league scorer with 20, followed by Sergio Aguero on 17 and Edin Dzeko, who managed 16.

With the Carabao Cup already in the bag, this was the first time City had won two trophies in one season since 1970, an outstanding return for manager Manuel Pellegrini after less than a year in charge.

Indeed, it represented a huge personal triumph for the Chilean, with this his first league title success in European football. He also became the first non-European manager to lift the Premier League.

"I'm so happy for the manager because it's his first title in Europe," Nasri, who had thrived under Pellegrini's watch, declared afterwards. "He remained calm. It was a pleasure to work for him. It's an amazing feeling. It's my second league in three years. It was an amazing league all year. Everyone put his ego on the side."

Pellegrini had altered City's style, with some of the conservatism that defined our play under former manager Roberto Mancini dispensed with and the handbrake removed. He had also restored harmony after an uneasy 2012-13 season.

This was exactly what the owners had wanted: a City side that could play beautiful attacking football and win major trophies.

"It was my first season in the Premier League, and I had to change a lot of things," Pellegrini revealed in the aftermath of the win over West Ham.

"The most important thing was we changed absolutely the way this team play. I am not criticising other styles or comparing. I like to play one way, and, for me, it was very important to give the reasons and to have the trust of the players to change the way they played before. When I arrived at this club maybe the relations between the squad were not in the best moment so I think it was very important to have calm and try to convince all of them how we can play and how it was

important to be very close – all of us, managers, players and fans – to try to win a very difficult title.

"I think the way we played was as important as winning the title. We have players to play on the counterattack but, for me, to win titles just in that way, I will not be happy. We won with 102 goals, and with the record of goals in all competitions in the history here in England. It is the way the team must play with the quality of players we have. It has been a brilliant season and I would say of all the sides we kept going the longest in all four competitions."

Kompany, the team's leader and club captain, only played in four of the first 13 Premier League games of the season after suffering groin and hamstring injuries, but his return to the side brought solidity and belief.

He was a key figure in our title triumph, and it was fitting he scored on the last day; a moment reminiscent of Tony Adams' final-day strike against Everton as Arsenal lifted the 1997-98 Premier League trophy.

"I'm extremely happy. It's unbelievable," Kompany declared afterwards. "This team has more than just talent – it has soul too. When we do well, I'm so happy for this club and the fans. It's a credit to how we've played this season.

"As a kid, all you dream of is lifting trophies and I'm achieving that now. We're building a club – not just a team. Next season, we need to be even better. If we want to be a big club, this trophy should be one of many."

Despite the obvious successes, the season still carried some regret. City were the best side in the county, and at one stage a first-ever English football treble looked a real possibility, but a disappointing FA Cup quarter-final defeat to Wigan Athletic, managed by former City striker Uwe Rosler, ended our hopes.

Privately, Pellegrini must have rued spurning an opportunity for further silverware, but publicly he described it as a blessing in disguise.

"The Wigan [FA Cup quarter-final] defeat was quite tough to bear but when you consider we played 14 or 15 more games than Liverpool, maybe if we had gone further in the FA Cup we may not be sitting here as champions," he said.

For Pellegrini, the celebrations would be short lived. His focus was on improving the side ahead of the 2014-15 season.

"I think it's very important to celebrate today and tomorrow and on Tuesday start working for next season," the Chilean asserted.

"We are going to do a balance of the whole year and the positive things and negative things and the way we can improve our squad. It has been a beautiful season, but you always need to continue winning and improving, and we are going to start working as soon as possible to be the strongest team next year."

Here's to you, Vincent Kompany.

CITY FOOTBALL ACADEMY

The style of Manchester City's football and the success we have enjoyed throughout the last decade has made us one of world football's most entertaining and respected teams - a side fans across the globe enjoy watching, regardless of allegiance.

But perhaps less well known is the dazzling transformation to the club's infrastructure during the same period.

At the heart of our off-field progress is the City Football Academy (CFA), opened in December 2014 after nearly six years of planning and development. It is the beating heart of Manchester City - a sustainable facility that places sporting and educational excellence at its centre and one that is now home to more than 170 male and female players from U9–U18.

It was inspired by His Highness Sheikh Mansour bin Zayed Al Nahyan, who laid out a clear vision. He wanted to create a focal point that would help the East Manchester community thrive, whilst also developing the best emerging young talent in the game.

Indeed, the CFA's ethos is to produce young footballers who are also well-rounded and well-educated young people.

It's an approach which is proving successful. City's Academy has brought through a series of impressive young talents, most notably Phil Foden, who is widely considered to be one of the best players in world football. He has been one of the main beneficiaries of the club's determination to offer a holistic and supportive environment for the stars of tomorrow.

And in 2020-21, City became the first club to achieve a hat-trick of Premier League titles in the same season as our Elite Development

Squad won PL2 and our U18s were crowned Under-18s Premier League National champions – supplementing the senior Premier League title Pep Guardiola's team secured.

"The function of City Football Academy is to produce young footballers for the future," Peter Bradshaw, Manchester City's Director of Sustainability, says. "We want to provide a well-trained, well-developed route from our academy into the first team, so we can grow our own players.

"Where players don't necessarily break into our first-team, have we created and developed and educated a person well enough for them to go and play elsewhere or get another career in football or elsewhere? That is the fundamental aim.

"In the process of helping them do that, we are helping young people gain a sense of community ethos so that we develop really good and really well-respected young footballers of the future that know where they have come from and understand their responsibilities."

The CFA - which is a stone's throw from the Etihad Stadium - sits at the heart of the Etihad Campus and two-thirds of the 16 pitches on site are dedicated to youth football. The wider development of the young players is supported by tailored coaching and education facilities, medical and sports science services, as well as player accommodation and parents' resources.

The comprehensive support on offer is all a part of the CFA's underlying ethos to provide as much help - and inspiration - as it can to those who use it.

It also helps inspire young players as they can literally see the stadium that they may someday grace with their own footballing talent.

"All the players and all the parents

that come on site can see the journey that is in front of them," Bradshaw adds. "There is a tangible link between the academy and the first team and young players can feel it and see it and almost touch it. We have built an aspirational place, where the whole sustainable journey can be maintained and enhanced."

The City Football Academy is an idea that has been replicated across the globe with the City Football Academy Melbourne opening in February 2015 followed by the Etihad City Football Academy New York in April 2018 and then, in March 2021, the Montevideo City Football Academy, the very first of its kind in South America.

They are all following in the footsteps of the first academy, a facility that has become a byword for success as well as sustainability with Manchester City

Premier League 2

at the forefront of the fight against climate change.

"We wanted to develop a truly sustainable project in every sense - from responsibly developing young people to helping create real, incredible regeneration for the whole area," Bradshaw explains. "The most important aspect for us was to generate real social value, providing

local jobs, using and buying local products and helping to improve the health and wellbeing of our young players but also our workforce and the local area."

The CFA is a prime example of taking an idea - a dream - and turning it into reality.

It has already nurtured thousands of young people, provided employment

opportunities to the local community and truly installed itself into the heart of East Manchester. Its impact and its benefit continue to grow by the day and, in the words of Brian Marwood, Managing Director of Global Football, it motivates and energises the entire City Football Group.

"It never fails to inspire me," Marwood says.

"So many people have played a huge part in this project, and it is so exciting to be involved in this. I'm proud of the people we have working here and the energy they provide every day. It is inspirational."

Roma 0-2 City

NASRI AND ZABALETA COMPLETE REMARKABLE TURNAROUND

10 December 2014

City went into Matchday 6 of our 2014/15 Champions League campaign needing a win in Rome to qualify as runners up in Group E. Bayern Munich were already through as group winners. City, Roma and CSKA Moscow all entered the final round of matches level on five points apiece.

Having taken two points from our first four group games, it was remarkable Manuel Pellegrini's side still had an opportunity of qualifying for the last-16. A dramatic 3-2 win over Bayern Munich in our previous home game had kept us alive, staving off the threat of a third group-stage exit in four seasons.

But this was a fixture full of potential pitfalls. City had never won a European game in Italy, and Roma were a side packed full of quality, with the likes of Radja Nainggolan, Miralem Pjanic, Francesco Totti and Daniele De Rossi in their squad. The atmosphere inside the Stadio Olimpico was famously hostile, amid the swirling noise of firecrackers and passionate Italian supporters. A win was by no means guaranteed.

"We had to meet the police in Rome three hours before kick-off and get busses to the stadium," explains Mike Hammond, a City season ticket holder for more than 25 years. "When we got to the stadium, it was a great atmosphere, loads of flares, big crowd, really noisy –

all the things you imagine Italian football to be."

To make matters worse, City were depleted. Captain Vincent Kompany was left out as a precaution after he failed a late fitness test, midfield driving force Yaya Touré was suspended, while principal goalscorer Sergio Aguero had knee ligament damage and David Silva was restricted to a place on the bench.

But City delivered perhaps our most accomplished Champions League performance since first qualifying in 2011 to win 2-0; a coming-of-age display that suggested we had learned some tough lessons in our three previous seasons in the competition.

It was a collective effort too. From Joe Hart in goal through to Edin Dzeko, who led the line superbly at the sharp end of the attack, everyone played their part.

Samir Nasri scored our first on the hour mark, lashing the ball home in off the post from the edge of the area. It was a venomous drive that left Roma 'keeper Morgan De Sanctis with no chance and was perhaps the best goal the Frenchman scored for City.

The Italian side had chances. Hart produced a fine stop to deny Kostas Manolas, and Martin Demichelis cleared one off the line, before Pablo Zabaleta struck from close range after Nasri's layoff to make it 2-0. The Argentine's celebration would immediately become an iconic part of Club folklore as he ran

to the away section kissing the City badge on his shirt. The travelling Mancunians were delirious.

The turnaround was complete. After ending the first four games without a win, victories over Bayern Much at home and Roma away had somehow sealed our passage into the knock-out phase.

"We were under quite a lot of pressure, particularly in the first half," says Hammond. "But then Nasri scored a cracker, but the cherry on the cake was Zaba scoring the second. There were incredible scenes in the away end, especially when Zaba ran straight over to us. It kind of looked like he couldn't believe he'd scored such an important goal, and neither could we! We were ridiculously happy, especially because it was Zaba, it always meant so much when he scored.

"It was City's first win in Italy and we were

there to see it. It was special, and obviously we qualified that night. We were locked in the stadium for about 90 minutes after the game and most of it was spent singing about Pablo!"

"I know how important the game was, not just for the team, but for the Club and the fans as well," Zabaleta said. "That's why, when I scored, I went to them straight away. I wanted to thank them for coming all the way to Rome to support us."

Pellegrini, clearly relieved, admitted afterwards he had delivered some harsh words to his players after the defeat to Roma at the Etihad.

"Before the game, I spoke with the players and I told them I thought we played the worst game of the season against Roma in Manchester," he said.

RAHEEM STERLING

Raheem Sterling joined City in 2015, a year before Pep Guardiola's arrival as manager. He scored 11 in 47 games in his first season, including a hat-trick in a 5-1 win over Bournemouth, as City won the League Cup and reached the Champions League semi-finals yet struggled in the Premier League. It was a mixed campaign and a steep learning curve for the young forward.

Under Guardiola's watchful eye, he has improved rapidly.

Where once Sterling was perhaps profligate in the final third, he is now a deadly forward player, with his pace, strength, tireless running, intelligence and finishing ability combining to create one of Europe's top marksmen.

The 2016-17 season saw him have direct involvement in 30 goals (scoring 10 and assisting 20), as his all-round game began to develop.

But it was the following season he really began to take off.

He scored 23 and assisted 17 in 46 games as City won the Premier League and League Cup. We set a string of records en route to the title, including becoming the first team in the history of English football to post a top-flight total of 100 points, registering a record 19-point winning margin. Sterling scored a series of decisive winners, against Bournemouth, Huddersfield, Southampton and Newcastle, without which our success would not have been possible.

And in 2018-19, he scored 25 and assisted 18 in 51 games as we became the first English side to win a clean-sweep of domestic honours in a single season.

He's blossomed into one of Europe's finest attacking talents and one of England's most important players.

In six years at City, his raw numbers tell an impressive tale: 114 goals and 87 assists in 292 games, winning three Premier League titles, an FA Cup and five League Cups along the way.

Only four English players have scored more goals in the Champions League than he has. At just 26, he could easily catch Frank Lampard, Paul Scholes, Steven Gerrard and Wayne Rooney and move into top spot.

"Raheem has been so important in the period since we arrived," Guardiola says. "Nothing we have done so far would have been possible without him."

There's little doubt he's been a key figure at club level for some time and, potentially, his best years lie ahead.

And in the summer on 2021, with predictable question marks surrounding his inclusion in the squad before the tournament began, Sterling was England's best player as they reached their first major final since 1966. Named in the Euro 2020 Team of the Tournament, he was a revelation and helped propel England to heights rarely seen.

But it isn't just on the field Sterling has proven influential. In June 2021, he was awarded an MBE for services to Racial Equality in Sport in the Queen's Birthday Honours list having become an extremely powerful voice in the campaign to highlight racial inequality in sport. He has been one of the leading figures in support of the Black Lives Matter movement – as well as for initiatives such as the United Nations' #FightRacism campaign – and has launched his own foundation aimed at helping disadvantaged young people.

"Receiving this honour is a fantastic feeling – I know it's something my family and friends will be truly proud of," he said after receiving the award.

He's a truly remarkable man, as well as a world-class footballer.

SOUTH STAND EXPANSION: THE NUMBERS	
45%	of employees from Greater Manchester
10%	of employees from East Manchester
5%	employed directly out of unemployment
39	apprentices hosted at the project
20	of the roles were work experience placements
4,600	hours of training delivered on site
21	trainees achieved full-time employment as a result of the expansion project
1,400	Local students engaged in the projects

City 3-0 Chelsea

CITY DESTROY CHELSEA IN FRONT OF NEW SOUTH STAND

16 August 2015

City sent out a resounding message to the rest of the Premier League in just the second game of the new 2015/16 season with a superb 3-0 win over reigning champions Chelsea at the Etihad.

Manuel Pellegrini's side were in sparkling form and goals from Sergio Aguero, Vincent Kompany and Fernandinho sealed a memorable victory as we outclassed Jose Mourinho's visitors.

The win saw City lead the way in the embryonic Premier League table, having taken six points from six.

City made a strong start and carved out two chances inside the first 30 seconds, Chelsea 'keeper Asmir Begovic denying Aguero after he latched on to David Silva's fine throughball, before Jesus Navas fired wide from the rebound.

Begovic saved from Aguero twice more but the Argentine finally opened the scoring after half an hour.

And he did so expertly, collecting Silva's pass and playing a quick one-two with Yaya Touré, before turning John Terry and striking home.

City created a plethora of chances, with Begovic producing an outstanding display, and Chelsea had to wait until the 70th minute for their first shot on target.

Our dominance was underlined when Kompany headed home from Silva's corner with 12 minutes remaining, and

Fernandinho's powerful drive sealed the win seven minutes later.

"To play against Chelsea is always very difficult - they defend with a lot of players and are fast on the counter-attack," Pellegrini said afterwards.

"But today we made a complete game, not only because we scored three goals but in the first 45 minutes we could have scored three more. Only the great performance of Asmir Begovic was the reason why we couldn't.

"We played in the way I like, to always try to score more. It was a great performance."

The game also saw the impressive new Etihad South Stand opened for the very first time.

The expansion saw an additional 6,250 seats in the new tier and 1,500 seats around the pitch, taking the Etihad's capacity to around 55,000.

As part of the unveiling, supporters took their seats 15 minutes before kick-off as giant banners rotated 90 degrees to reveal the new stand in dramatic fashion.

The construction of the new tier – including roof, corporate suites and new seating – involved 3,010 tonnes of steelwork as well as precast concrete terracing.

Each phase of the stadium expansion process created new construction jobs and additional match day roles, bringing a direct benefit to the local community in Manchester.

KEVIN DE BRUYNE

Kevin De Bruyne's rise to the top of world football has been remarkable. Widely considered the finest midfielder in the game, his CV is glittering, a plethora of personal awards and team prizes to his name.

The recognition is more than justified. We are now looking at one of the greatest players of this generation, one central to City winning three Premier League titles, one FA Cup and five League Cups. This summer, he became only the third player to win back-to-back PFA Player of the Year awards, following Thierry Henry and Cristiano Ronaldo. He's also collected one UEFA Midfielder of the Season prize, been named in the PFA Premier League Team of the Year on three occasions and the FIFPRO World XI once.

He came to City having impressed in Germany, firstly on loan at Werder Bremen for a season, before a brilliant 18-month period with Wolfsburg, which saw him become one of the best players in the Bundesliga.

The move to City in the summer of 2015 ignited further improvement. Since arriving in English football, he's been on a quest to become the finest creative force in the league. As it stands today, it's mission accomplished.

He's played 262 matches, scored 67 goals and assisted 107. He's an icon, a player who unites fans of all colours in their admiration, the standard bearer for central-midfielders. "Apart from Ronaldo and Messi I think he is the best in the world," Jack Grealish says. "He has got absolutely everything."

His debut season under Manuel Pellegrini saw him score 16 and assist 13 – healthy numbers and an indication of what was to follow. He won the club's Etihad Player of the Year award and the fans were in no doubt we had a star in the making.

Pep Guardiola's first season in charge saw a period of transition, but the Centurions campaign of 2017-18 saw him excel, his iconic winning goal away at Chelsea signalling a shift in mentality. "That, I think, was the first day we believed in ourselves, me included, to say, okay, we can go away on the biggest stage and win," Guardiola says. He ended the season by assisting Gabriel Jesus' winner at Southampton to seal 100 Premier League points and again picked up the club's Etihad Player of the Year award.

"He's a masterclass player, one of the best I have ever trained in my life," was Guardiola's assessment.

His Fourmidables season was disrupted by injury, but he still managed 32 appearances, scoring six and assisting 11, including a wonderful cameo in the FA Cup final against Watford that saw him score one and set another up in a 35-minute masterclass.

But perhaps his best seasons have been the last two. He's been sensational, his reputation as the best in the Premier League cemented, with City winning one Premier League title and two League Cups, as well as reaching our first ever Champions League final.

De Bruyne has given City fans six years of brilliance. He signed a new deal in April 2021, extending his stay until the summer of 2025, by which time he'll have spent a decade at the club. "Since joining City in 2015, I have felt at home," he says. "I love the fans, my family are settled here in Manchester and my own game has developed really well."

It's been a pleasure watching him go from one of Europe's most promising young players to a consistent, world-class operator. He's one of the very best in world football and we are lucky enough to call him our own.

Crystal Palace 0-1 City

DE BRUYNE MAKES DEBUT AS KELECHI BAGS LATE WINNER

12 September 2015

For some players who arrive in the Premier League, it can take time for them to show their true ability. A period of adaptation is needed while they adjust to the pace, physicality and tactics of a league unlike any other in world football.

For others you instantly get a feel for what they are about. They don't necessarily perform at their best straight away, but you immediately have a sense of their skillset and what they will offer.

Kevin De Bruyne, who made his City debut away at Crystal Palace early in the 2015-16 season, fell firmly into the latter category. He came on after 25 minutes, replacing the injured Sergio Aguero, and within minutes had demonstrated his vision and passing quality. Few players see the game quite as clearly as the Belgian.

City won the match 1-0, maintaining our 100 per cent start to the season that had seen us take 15 points from the first 15 available, becoming just the fourth team to open an English top-flight campaign with five clean sheets. Kelechi Iheanacho was the hero at Selhurst Park, scoring his first City goal in the dying seconds.

At 18 years and 344 days old, Iheanacho became the third youngest player to score for City in the Premier League after Micah Richards and Daniel Sturridge.

It was a dream moment for the youngster, who had shown enough during his time in City's Academy, as well as on pre-season tours of Australia, Vietnam and Germany, to justify his chance.

"He's just 18 and started working with our squad last season, but he was unlucky and had a big injury in the last three months of the season," manager Manuel Pellegrini said.

"This year he started pre-season with the squad and will be a very important player for the future. He's one of the reasons I didn't bring another striker in when we sold Edin Dzeko. He deserves that chance."

Iheanacho's goal spared Jesus Navas' blushes, the Spanish winger having missed a gilt-edged chance in the second half when he collected De Bruyne's pass, rounded Palace 'keeper Alex McCarthy but missed the target with his weaker foot.

Palace will feel unlucky not to have taken something from the game. They created a number of chances. Yannick Bolasie forced a decent save from Joe Hart and Dwight Gayle could perhaps have scored before Iheanacho's winner.

The injury to Aguero was a huge blow – he was in outstanding form – but the performance of De Bruyne offered plenty to be excited about. It was a precursor to what City fans were about to enjoy in the coming years.

The big question, though, was whether City could maintain the perfect start to the season that had seen us go five points clear at the top of the table after five matches.

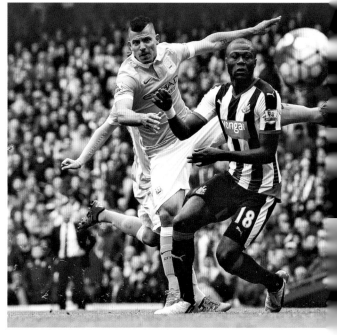

City 6-1 Newcastle United
FIVE-STAR AGUERO CREATES HISTORY
3 October 2015

Sergio Aguero had quickly established a reputation as one of the finest goalscorers in Premier League history.

In his first four seasons as a Manchester City player, he had scored 107 goals in all competitions, helping us to two Premier League titles and a League Cup. He was, undoubtedly, one of the most feared strikers in the English game.

But going into our home match with Newcastle United in October of his fifth season, Aguero had only scored once in the Premier League in the first seven games of the campaign. The Argentine was without a goal in open play in 595 minutes in all competitions, and any Premier League goal in 424 minutes since City's win over Chelsea on 16 August.

All that changed after a remarkable five goals in 20 minutes against Newcastle, a virtuoso performance that showcased his outstanding instincts in front of goal and saw him join an elite list of players who had scored five times in a single Premier League game.

Newcastle had gone ahead when Aleksandar Mitrovic scored his first goal for the club, but it was a mere bump in the road for City, as Aguero took centre stage and delivered a striker's masterclass.

The Argentine was only on the pitch for 66 minutes, being taken off early by City manager Manuel Pellegrini as a precaution after the striker had received treatment at half-time. If he had remained on, Aguero would almost certainly have added to his extraordinary five-goal haul.

Remarkably, his five goals came in a ridiculous 20-minute period either side of half-time, as he joined Dimitar Berbatov, Jermain Defoe, Andy Cole and Alan Shearer as the only players to have scored five in a single Premier League game. Defoe's record for being the quickest to score five (36 minutes) had been obliterated in the process.

"Aguero was world class," Newcastle manager Steve McClaren said after the game. "He is getting back to form, and we were punished by a really high-quality opponent."

His first, after 42 minutes, was a close-range diving header. David Silva played a wonderful ball to the back post, Fernandinho nodded across the six-yard box and Aguero was there to finish expertly. Right place; right time.

Then came a dazzling spell after the break – goals arriving on 49, 50, 60 and 62 minutes – that left Newcastle dizzy and without any hope of a recovery.

Each one demonstrated his instincts: a deflected left-footed strike, a delightful first-time chip, a powerful curling drive into the bottom corner from the edge of the area and a back post poacher's finish.

In between that flurry of goals, Kevin De Bruyne found time to score perhaps the goal of the day, a brilliant over-the-shoulder volley.

It was a fine win for City, who were without Yaya Touré and Vincent Kompany, with the victory sending us top of the table after eight games.

"Sergio Aguero is different," Pellegrini said. "In other games he was maybe having a lot of chances but not scoring – today he returned to his normal amount of chances he creates, but this time he scored.

"He was not upset about going off. He was having treatment at half-time and it was a risk for him to finish the whole game."

A stunning individual performance from a player developing a reputation as the best striker on the planet.

Liverpool 1-1 City
(City win 3-1 on penalties)

CABALLERO SEALS CULT HERO STATUS AS CITY WIN LEAGUE CUP

28 February 2016

Willy Caballero wrote his name into City folklore with a match-winning display at Wembley as City beat Jurgen Klopp's Liverpool to win the League Cup for the second time in three seasons.

The 34-year-old goalkeeper was given the nod to start ahead of first-choice Joe Hart, a move which caused some consternation before kick-off given Caballero had endured a tough and testing afternoon the weekend before at Chelsea in an FA Cup tie.

But Caballero made a remarkable stop from Divock Origi's header in extra-time, before then producing three penalty saves in the shoot-out – from Lucas, Philippe Coutinho and Adam Lallana – to win the cup in spectacular fashion for City.

In truth, City should not have been drawn into a shoot-out, such were the quality of chances we created in the 90 minutes. Fernandinho, who played on the right side of midfield, scored just after half-time to give Manuel Pellegrini's men a deserved lead, and Raheem Sterling missed two glorious opportunities.

But Coutinho equalised for Liverpool with seven minutes of normal time remaining to take the game into extra-time.

Emre Can scored Liverpool's first penalty in the ensuing shoot-out – but Caballero would not be beaten thereafter. Fernandinho hit the post with City's first penalty, before Jesus Navas and Sergio Aguero both scored. Yaya Touré, always the man for the big occasion, then stepped up and took the decisive kick that saw City over the line.

As is the way with modern managers, Pellegrini utilised his second-choice goalkeeper in cup competitions – it's a way of enticing a high-quality understudy to the club and keeping them sharp throughout the season in case they are called upon.

But when a team reaches a showpiece final, the question of 'head vs heart' always emerges.

Pellegrini went with his heart, a particularly difficult decision given the Argentine stopper had conceded five at Chelsea a week earlier, but his faith was rewarded on a day Caballero became a City cult hero.

"I'd rather lose a final than my word," Pellegrini said afterwards when asked what made him choose Caballero after the difficult time he had endured away at Stamford Bridge.

Vincent Kompany was City's best player on the day, producing a heroic captain's performance at the back, the latest example of his talismanic leadership qualities.

"I was concerned about the amount of chances we missed," added Pellegrini. "After that we played better in extra-time.

"It's a very important moment, and it's always very special to win a title at Wembley."

With City still in the hunt for Premier League and Champions League success, could this win be the launchpad for bigger prizes?

City 1-0 Paris Saint-Germain

PELLEGRINI GUIDES CITY INTO FIRST CHAMPIONS LEAGUE SEMI-FINAL

12 April 2016

For all the progress City had made on the domestic front in recent seasons, the European platform had provided an altogether more difficult challenge.

Two group-stage exits under Roberto Mancini were followed by two last-16 defeats, both at the hands of Barcelona, in Manuel Pellegrini's first two years in charge.

But the 2015-16 season had seen real progress. City topped a difficult Group D containing Juventus, Sevilla and Borussia Moenchengladbach, before cruising past Dynamo Kiev in the last-16 thanks to a 3-1 aggregate win. Already in uncharted territory, a 2-2 draw in Paris in the first leg of our quarter-final tie with PSG, who had already wrapped up the Ligue 1 title, had set things up beautifully for the return game in Manchester.

What followed was a demonstration of City's growing maturity on the European stage.

Joe Hart was exceptional, making a trio of important saves, including two from thumping Zlatan Ibrahimovic free-kicks. Sergio Aguero constantly frightened the PSG defence and had chances, including when he won and then missed a penalty in the first half.

Ultimately, it was Kevin De Bruyne who scored the only goal of the game 15 minutes from time, taking one touch to set himself before curling a beauty from 20 yards into the bottom corner. The Belgian was improving all the time, becoming one of the most productive creative forces in European football, and had now had a hand in 27 goals in

all competitions for City this season (15 goals, 12 assists).

City defended superbly and were the better side, deservedly seeing the job through as Pellegrini became the first man to lead City to a European semi-final since 1971 when Joe Mercer guided us through to the last four of the European Cup Winners' Cup against Chelsea.

There were 53,039 packed into the Etihad and the atmosphere was electric, but rather than be overawed by the magnitude of the occasion, City rose to it. The noise the fans made at the full-time whistle said everything: this was a hugely important night in Manchester City's history.

For manager Pellegrini, who knew he would be replaced in the summer by Pep Guardiola, it was essential for him to have improved City's Champions League pedigree.

"I came to City because I had good performances in Europe, so to leave this club without taking them to a new state would have been a bad thing for me," he said.

"It is very important to me to be in the semi-finals because that is my job.

"It is a very great achievement for the Club. It's not easy to be in the last four as there are great teams in Europe but every year we are improving.

"In the semi-finals you know you have to play against a very big team. But playing the way we did here, we have a lot of chance against anyone."

City were in the hat for the Champions League semi-final draw three days later, with everyone focused on reaching the final in Milan on 28 May.

PEP GUARDIOLA

The appointment of Pep Guardiola in the summer of 2016 caused huge excitement across City's fanbase. And rightly so.

He arrived with a stellar record, his status as a modern-day great secure having won 21 major trophies in seven years as a manager (four at Barcelona and three at Bayern Munich). In the eyes of the club's owners, this was the man to take City to a new level.

And so it has proved. Guardiola has overseen a golden period for City, ushering in an era of sustained success unprecedented in the Club's 127-year history.

In his five full seasons as manager, City have won three Premier League titles, one FA Cup, four League Cups, two Community Shields and reached a Champions League final for the first time in our history.

The visionary Catalan has also presided over a stunning array of new records, including helping City become the first side in English Premier League history to claim 100 points in a season (2017-18) and guiding the club to all four English domestic trophies in 2018-19.

Those remarkable achievements have further cemented Guardiola's status as one of football's greatest-ever managers – and as one of the titanic figures in City history. His 10 major trophies since joining City mean he has now won 31 since entering management in 2008. It's a quite remarkable record.

"He's one of the best coaches of all time," says Ilkay Gundogan. "It was an achievement for me to play for him, to train under him, being able to learn from Pep is amazing."

But it isn't just the results he has delivered. City play with wonderful style, defined by our ability to keep the ball, to complete intricate passing moves and weave bewitching patterns across the pitch. Guardiola's ideals

and aesthetic are now welded into the club's philosophy.

"It is testament to the qualities of the man that Pep Guardiola's passion and intelligent approach are now woven into the very fabric of the football we play and our culture as a club," Chairman Khaldoon Al Mubarak said when Guardiola signed a new contract in November 2020. "That impact has been central to our success during his tenure and it is why I am delighted that he shares our view that there is so much more to be achieved both on and off the field."

Guardiola's presence also attracts the finest footballers. He carries a gravitas few can match and players want to be touched by his genius. "When you have the opportunity to be trained by Guardiola, you don't say no," says Bernardo Silva. It means City have a vast array of talent, a squad full of depth and quality, capable of competing aggressively on all fronts.

The continued excellence of City under Pep is underlined by the fact we have now won ten of the past 15 major English trophies available. And in the 2020-21 season, with a schedule that was draining due to the difficulties posed by the COVID-19 pandemic, our guiding principles of reinvention, resilience and teamwork saw us create a series of new and notable record-breaking achievements, including a remarkable run of 21 consecutive wins in all competitions between December and March and 19 consecutive away wins across all competitions – both top-flight English records.

Guardiola's desire, passion, ideas and obsession with the game mark him out as a true genius. Inspired by the great Johan Cruyff, he has taken the learnings from his mentor and reinvented the game.

Manchester City are proud to call him our manager.

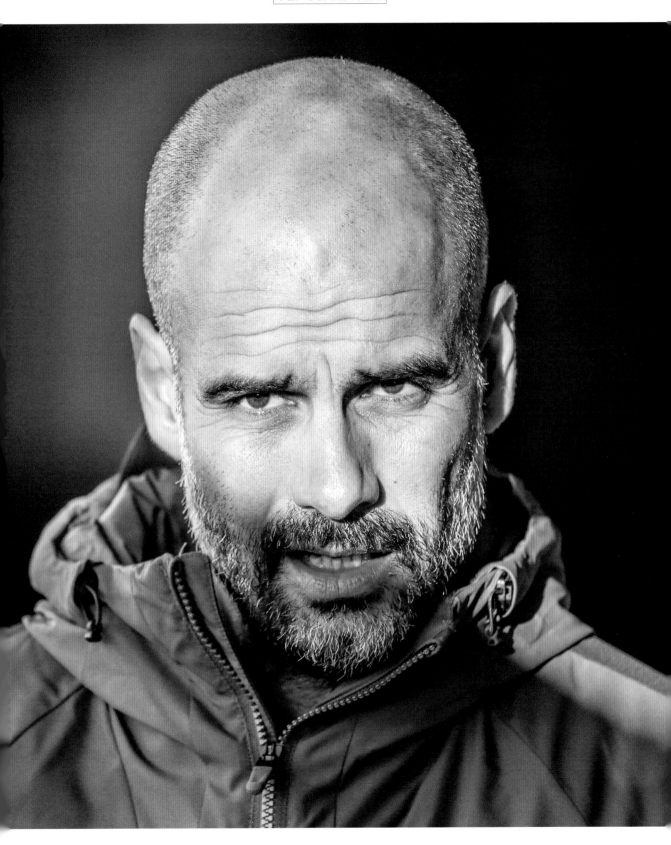

PEP GUARDIOLA
Managerial statistics

Games	294
Won	215
Drawn	36
Lost	43
Goals For	714
Goals against	240
Goals difference	474
Win Percentage %	73.1%
Trophies	10
Games per trophy	29.4
Start date	01/07/2016
End Date	28/07/2021
Total days	1853

SIGNIFICANT PREMIER LEAGUE MILESTONES SET UNDER GUARDIOLA

Most points in a season	100
Most wins in a season	32
Most home wins in a season	18
Most away wins in a season	16
Most consecutive wins	18
Most consecutive away wins	11
Biggest title-winning margin	19
Most goals	106
Best goal difference	+79

ILKAY GUNDOGAN

Ilkay Gundogan was Pep Guardiola's first signing as Manchester City manager, and it's easy to see why the German midfielder was so high on his list of initial targets. Few players in City's recent history keep the ball as well as Gundogan, and with possession high on the list of Guardiola's footballing ideals, a player like Gundogan is a vital element of his setup.

But Gundogan has much more to his game than ball retention. He is incredibly versatile, capable of playing both deep-lying and advanced midfield roles, as well as in a False 9 position. He operates in them all expertly, making him a precious commodity to Guardiola during a long season where he needs solutions to the myriad questions posed by our opponents.

Perhaps the first time most City fans had seen Gundogan up close was when Borussia Dortmund visited the Etihad in the 2012 Champions League group stage. The German side completely outplayed City, and but for a heroic display by Joe Hart would have beaten us comfortably. Gundogan was outstanding, a metronomic presence in the Dortmund midfield and seemingly impossible to dispossess.

He had won one Bundesliga title and one DFB-Pokal during his time with Dortmund – and reached the final of the Champions League in 2013 – but the lure of Guardiola and the challenge of adapting to the Premier League convinced him to make the switch.

He arrived at City in the summer of 2016 having had significant injury problems. A back problem kept him out for almost the entire 2013-14 season, and he had suffered a dislocated kneecap a month before joining City in a freak training ground accident. He made his debut in September 2016 and bagged his first double away at West Brom in late October. Three days later he scored another brace, this time in a famous win over Barcelona, his influence beginning to grow.

But his rotten luck with injuries continued. A collision with Watford's Nordin Amrabat in December saw him suffer anterior cruciate ligament damage. He got up from the incident and convinced club doctor Max Sala he could continue. But moments later, he came off the field in tears, his season over.

For a player to suffer one injury that threatens a career is bad enough. Three is simply unfair. He went for surgery in Barcelona under the watchful eye of Dr. Ramon Cugat.

He played 49 times in all competitions during the 2017-18 season as City won the Premier League with 100 points and 50 the following year as we won all four major English honours in the same season. To play 99 matches in the two years after such a major injury was testament to Gundogan's resilience and mental strength, as well as the club's medical staff.

But the 2020-21 season was perhaps the pinnacle of his time at City. Used in a multitude of positions – often our furthest player forward – he scored 17 goals in 46 games as we won the Premier League and League Cup against the backdrop of a relentless fixture schedule. He was remarkable, a leader on and off the field.

In total, he's played 210 games for City, scoring 39. He has won three Premier League titles, an FA Cup and four League Cups.

Given the difficulties he faced in his first year, it's an incredible return for one of the most thoughtful, intelligent footballers in the modern game.

PHIL FODEN

There are few finer sights in football than that of a local lad playing for the team they grew up supporting.

For the fans, they see their own dreams being fulfilled on the pitch by one of their own. For the player, it's the realisation of a lifelong ambition.

Phil Foden has achieved just that, following in a long line of City academy starlets who have gone on to play for our first team. From ballboy at the Etihad to the fulcrum of City's creative set.

The difference, of course, with Foden's transition to the City senior setup when compared with many academy graduates across our history is he has fought his way into a squad containing world-class quality from top to bottom. In every position, you must dislodge one of the best players in Europe if you want to get a game. Foden, to his eternal credit, has managed to do it.

Indeed, that level of competition has been a blessing to a player as gifted as Foden. He had David Silva to study at close quarters, probably the greatest creative force in Premier League history. Able to train with the great Spanish midfielder on a day-to-day basis, watching the way he lived his life and prioritised his profession, Foden had the ideal blueprint laid out before his very eyes.

"Silva is my idol really," a 17-year-old Foden said when first training alongside the City legend during our tour of the US in the summer of 2017. "I try and watch what he does and learn from him and try and do the same things."

It worked. Foden, who joined City's academy as a nine-year-old, made his debut in November 2017, replacing Yaya Touré as a late substitute against Feyenoord. Two weeks later, he made his first start against Shakhtar Donetsk, which saw him become the youngest English player, at the age of 17 years and 192 days, to start in a Champions League match – and the first player born in the 2000s to do so.

And by the end of that season, he had become the youngest ever Premier League winner, his five appearances in our title-winning campaign enough to earn him a medal.

Fast-forward three years and Foden is now considered one of the best young players in world football. He's already won 10 major honours and played well over 100 games for City, scoring many memorable goals. In terms of natural talent and ability, few in the game can hold a candle to him.

A keen fisherman away from the pitch, his favourite pastime has provided him with a way of escaping the stresses and tensions that come with professional football. "It's good for clearing your head after you've had a bad game," Foden says. "I've found it the solution to everything."

He remains proud of his Stockport roots and has been seen many times playing street football with youngsters in the area. "I've still got family around Stockport, so I go and visit sometimes, and kids are just starstruck to see me," he explains. "It's quite strange because I was one of those kids and was just the same as them. It's good to play with them and see a smile on their face."

City and England's futures are in safe hands. Foden, a father to young Ronnie, is a family man, humble and grounded, with an outstanding work ethic. Throw in his outrageous technical quality and it's a winning formula.

LEROY SANÉ

In terms of raw talent and natural ability, there are very few players in City's recent history who can match Leroy Sané. He makes the game look easy, with balance, poise, pace and outstanding technique combining to lethal effect.

In his four years at City, the winger won seven trophies, playing 135 times and scoring 39 goals. Those are, undoubtedly, impressive numbers for a wide player, but it was the unquantifiable elements that City fans will remember the most about Sané's contribution: the beauty of his game, the gracious pirouettes, the nutmegs and the ease with which he would go past defenders.

He descends from a family of rich sporting heritage. His mother, Regina Weber, won a bronze medal in gymnastics at the 1984 Olympics in Los Angeles, while his father, Souleymane, was a professional footballer who played for FC Nurnberg and SG Wattenscheid.

"My parents taught me a lot," he says. "I have the movements from my mother and speed from my father."

The German joined City in the summer of 2016 and was initially eased into the side by Pep Guardiola. But that changed in December of his first season when he produced an explosive man of the match display in a 2-1 win over Arsenal at the Etihad. A watershed afternoon, it lit the blue touch paper for Sané, with all the flashes of brilliance we had seen in the weeks leading up the game coming into full bloom.

His second season saw him take off and affirm his status as one of Europe's best young players. He scored 14 goals in all competitions and assisted a further 17 as City won the Premier League with a record 100 points and won the Carabao Cup. He ended the 2017-18 season by being awarded the PFA Young Player of the Year prize.

Sané was lethal throughout the campaign, his pace used to frightening effect and his starting position, tight to the left-hand touchline, stretching teams, creating space infield for the likes of Kevin De Bruyne, David Silva and Sergio Aguero to exploit. With many of City's players focused on short, sharp passing, Sané was often the catalyst for a more direct approach; a change of pace that opposition teams found unsettling.

We were looking at a player in full flight, fuelled by the precociousness of youth and augmented by his outrageous natural talent. His teammates knew just how gifted he was. They would regularly crack a wry smile when Sané's name was mentioned, before delivering a shake of the head to express their almost disbelief at his quality.

Sané was once again central to our success during the Fourmidables campaign of 2018-19, playing 47 matches, scoring 16 and assisting 18 as we became the first team to win a clean-sweep of all four major English honours in a single season.

But the 2019-20 season proved to be his last. He was injured in the opening stages of the Community Shield, damaging the anterior cruciate ligament in his right knee. After a painstaking recovery, he made one more appearance for City as a late substitute in a 5-0 win over Burnley, before moving to Bayern Munich in the summer of 2020.

He may have only spent four seasons at City, one of which was wiped out through injury, but he made a significant impact. Sané was an entertainer, an off-the-cuff wide man who could hug the touchline or drift inside and cause havoc. He was, quite simply, a joy to watch.

JOHN STONES

"After all the memories that I have already made – the good times, the people – I feel like this is definitely home," John Stones said after signing a new five-year contract in August 2021, a deal that will see him clock up a decade at the club.

His fresh commitment completed an incredible renaissance for the 26-year-old. A year earlier, there were serious question marks about his City future. He was in and out of Pep Guardiola's first XI and out of the international frame. Fast forward 12 months and he was one of our outstanding players as we won the Premier League and League Cup, as well as reaching our first ever Champions League final, before producing seven immaculate performances for England at Euro 2020 as they qualified for their first major final since 1966.

Stones has delivered on his seemingly limitless potential. He started life at Barnsley, at the time one of the country's most forward-thinking academies, led by Ronnie Branson and Mark Burton, who were both inspired by watching Pep Guardiola's all-conquering Barcelona side.

Given licence to prioritise development over results, they encouraged playing out from the back, with centre-halves who step into midfield and take risks. Mentored by coaches with a modern view of the game and away from the glare of an elite Premier League academy, Stones was given the chance to indulge his creative side and he thrived. The result was a ball-playing centre-half unlike any England has produced since Rio Ferdinand.

Keith Hill gave him his Barnsley debut in March 2012 aged 17 and 28 appearances later he was transferred to Everton. He was superb in his three seasons at Goodison Park and when Guardiola took charge at City in the summer of 2016, he made Stones one of his primary targets, visiting the defender personally and spending two hours convincing him to sign.

His style fits Guardiola's perfectly. Stones is an excellent defender, first and foremost, but he has the kind of composure on the ball you would normally associate with a creative midfielder. He has no problem taking the ball off the goalkeeper, striding forward and playing a pass between the lines. It's magnificent to watch.

And the City fans have adopted him as a firm favourite. Social media is awash with Stones love on matchdays and the defender embraces it completely. "It is a love-love relationship," he says. "It is difficult when you can't thank them for the support face to face. It's something I don't take for granted.

"It would take a long time, but I can express it in interviews and over camera. When I am out in the pitch, I try to give them everything and I think you can just sense the relationship that we have."

Since joining City, he has provided Guardiola with an almost personal project. The manager has seen enough in Stones to stick with him, even during difficult periods for the defender on and off the pitch. His stylish play, quality on the ball and bravery in possession are all straight out of the Guardiola playbook. The manager has desperately wanted to help him succeed and the results are clear.

Stones has won three Premier League titles, one FA Cup and four League Cups. With his new deal signed and his confidence high, it seems likely he will only add to his impressive haul.

Manchester United 1-2 City

GUARDIOLA'S FIRST MANCHESTER DERBY ENDS IN FINE WIN

10 September 2016

Much like 2013, the summer of 2016 was one of significant change across Manchester. Pep Guardiola was officially installed as the new City boss on 1 July, and his old adversary, Jose Mourinho, took over at United. Given their clashes when Guardiola was at Barcelona and Mourinho was in charge at arch La Liga rivals Real Madrid, it was a dream narrative for media outlets.

The first Manchester derby – which arrived less than a month into the new season – was, therefore, highly anticipated.

It was Guardiola who came out on top, with City winning 2-1 at Old Trafford – the 50th time across all competitions we had beaten United.

First-half goals from Kevin De Bruyne and Kelechi Iheanacho, who finished off with glee in front of the Stretford End after De Bruyne had struck the post, deservedly put City 2-0 up.

With a goal and assist to his name, De Bruyne had now been directly involved in 32 goals in 46 appearances in all competitions for City.

But an error from Claudio Bravo – who had been recruited from Barcelona in the summer and installed as City's number one keeper – allowed Zlatan Ibrahimovic to narrow the deficit ahead of the break, with Mourinho also claiming Bravo should have been red carded for a tackle on Wayne Rooney after an initial heavy touch from the 'keeper.

Despite a period of second-half United pressure, City held firm though and could have had a third when De Bruyne struck the upright after collecting Leroy Sané's pass.

The result also meant City remained top of the table, having won all four Premier League games since Guardiola took charge. Mourinho had now won just three of his 17 meetings with Guardiola with six ending in draws and the Catalan enjoying success in the other eight.

"We are happy with the victory, and it was open until the end and so tough at Old Trafford," Guardiola reflected.

"In the first half we were better; they pushed us in the second half. It's just three points but for our confidence [it's good]."

With the only downside of the day the mistake by Bravo, Guardiola sought to offer a broader view of the goalkeeper's performance in his post-match press conference, explaining how the Chilean's ability on the ball helped his side create sustained build-up play from deep.

"We played good in the first half because of Claudio," Guardiola added. "I like the 'keepers to attack the ball and after what happened with the goal, in the second half he continued to play and that's a good thing about his personality."

And with City enjoying the majority of the ball, reducing United to their fourth lowest home possession figure in the Premier League since 2003-04 (39.9%), Guardiola said this was a fundamental aspect of his plan to turn his side into the best team in the Premier League.

"Until my last day in England I will try to play with the ball as much as possible," he stressed. "I know it's impossible for 90 minutes but, I'm sorry, I will not negotiate that.

"But we have only been together two months, so we have time to get better."

City 3-1 Barcelona

GUNDOGAN SCORES A BRACE ON FAMOUS NIGHT AT THE ETIHAD

1 November 2016

A visit of Barcelona, one of the most storied and successful teams in the history of European football, always sets pulses racing for football fans.

However, for City supporters it had also become a somewhat daunting affair.

We had lost all five of our previous Champions League assignments against them.

Twice the Catalans had eliminated us at the last-16 stage when Manuel Pellegrini was City manager, and in the reverse group fixture a month before this game at the Etihad, we had been beaten 4-0 at the Camp Nou, overwhelmed after a red card for goalkeeper Claudio Bravo.

In those five matches, we had conceded 10 goals and scored just two.

Perhaps understandably then, there were some nerves and trepidation going into this latest match-up, exacerbated by Lionel Messi scoring for Barcelona after 21 minutes – his 90th Champions League goal.

But there was a steely resolve about City on an atmospheric night in Manchester. And when Raheem Sterling capitalised on Sergi Roberto's mistake to set up Ilkay Gundogan for the equaliser, there was an explosion of noise from the Etihad stands.

From there it turned into a classic. City stepped up a gear; Barcelona struggled to cope.

Kevin de Bruyne curled a free-kick past Marc-Andre ter Stegen six minutes after the restart to put Pep Guardiola's side ahead and send the Etihad into delirium, with City now the dominant side.

Andre Gomes rattled the bar for Barcelona as they went in search of an equaliser, but with 16 minutes remaining, Gundogan, outstanding all evening, grabbed his second to seal a famous win.

It felt like a seismic night for City in a competition which hadn't been kind to us. De Bruyne was the best player on the pitch, Sterling was exceptional and should have had a penalty in the first half, and there was an intensity about City's play that was encouraging.

"They had an amazing 30 minutes, we had a lot of problems, but our first goal helped us a lot," manager Pep Guardiola said afterwards, visibly delighted at the way City had played against his former side.

"In the second half we created a lot of counter attacks. I am so happy for the guys, it is the first time we have beaten the best team in the world."

It meant City had seven points from four matches in Group C, and a win at Borussia Moenchengladbach on Matchday 5 would seal progress to the last-16.

After five defeats that had seen City outplayed on each occasion, to produce such a high-octane performance against Barcelona felt like a significant moment.

"Today is a good step," was Guardiola's verdict. "We play against a great team, and we compete. Now they will realise: 'Wow, we won against the best team.'"

GABRIEL JESUS

Gabriel Jesus has achieved so much for one so young. He's still only 24, yet has won 12 major trophies in club football, 10 of them with City, and led Brazil to Copa America success. It's a quite remarkable record.

His rise has been rapid. In 2012, he was playing várzea, Brazilian grassroots football that takes place on poor quality clay pitches. By the time he signed for City in January 2017, his ascent from street footballer to the most talked about young South American in the game was complete.

Jesus grew up in Jardim Peri, a tough, uncompromising favela just outside of Sao Paulo. He was the youngest of four children raised by his mother, Vera Lucia, who worked as a housekeeper and remains his biggest influence to this day.

After a period with amateur side Associação Atlética Anhanguera, where he scored 54 goals in 48 appearances, things began to move more quickly when he joined Palmeiras' youth setup in 2013.

The young Jesus went on to break the club's academy goalscoring record, scoring 37 goals in 27 appearances in the Campeonato Paulista, Brazil's under-17 state championships in 2014. The calls for him to be included in the senior side grew rapidly.

After starring at the Under-20 World Cup in 2015, he became a regular for Palmeiras who went on to win the Copa de Brasil, Jesus' first major piece of silverware. His contribution was recognised when he was awarded the prestigious Golden Boy award at the end of his first season.

His second season in professional football could hardly have gone much better. Jesus became Brazil's No. 9 and led their South American World Cup qualifying group recovery. He

also agreed a deal to sign for City, a move he delayed so he could finish the job of helping Palmeiras win their first league title in 22 years.

From the streets of Jardim Peri to the star of Brazilian football, it was fairy-tale stuff.

Since joining City, winning trophies has become a habit. He scored in the dying seconds of our final game of

> "But it is the things he does for the team that people don't realise he does. He helps us with his pressing and he is a joyous guy"

the 2017-18 season to end his first full campaign in English football with a Premier League title and a goal that secured a record 100 points. His lob now stands alongside Paul Dickov's strike against Gillingham in 1999 and Sergio Aguero's winner vs QPR in 2012 in the pantheon of all-time dramatic Manchester City goals.

The following season Jesus scored the winner in the FA Cup semi-final and a brace in the final as City won all four domestic trophies, and in the summer of 2019, he scored in the final of the Copa America as Brazil secured the prestigious competition for the ninth time.

In total, he has scored 82 goals in 195 games for City.

"You cannot imagine how happy we are when Gabriel can score the goals he has scored," Pep Guardiola says. "But it is the things he does for the team that people don't realise he does. He helps us with his pressing and he is a joyous guy."

He's one of the most hard-working forwards in world football and is already a serial winner. The future looks bright for Gabriel Jesus.

BERNARDO SILVA

If anyone needs an example of what makes Bernardo Silva such a special player, they should watch City's 2-1 win over Liverpool in January 2019 for definitive evidence.

The midfielder's technical proficiency is obvious – he has quick feet, can produce skill in tight areas and has an eye for a pass – but the humility and selflessness with which he plays is what separates him from so many others. In that game against Liverpool, a crucial, must-win occasion, he ran a remarkable 13.7km, giving everything to ensure City came away with three points against our fiercest Premier League title rival.

This was Bernardo in a nutshell: a brilliant technician and one of the most altruistic players in the game.

"He did everything," Pep Guardiola said afterwards. "He is the smallest one, but he shows us that to play football, you don't have to be tall or more physical. He is incredible. I haven't seen a performance like that in a while."

Bernardo was educated in Teresinhas on the outskirts of central Lisbon, at a private school called Colegio Valsassina. Education, in his parents' eyes, came first. They wanted a well-rounded, intellectually stimulated son, but his love and passion of football was always bubbling to the surface. "My parents always liked that I played football and did what I loved to do," Bernardo says. "They always told me I could play football but that I must keep going with my studies."

A Benfica supporter throughout his life, he joined the Portuguese giant's academy aged seven. He spent 12 years there, impressing for their B side in the Segunda Division, and in the summer of 2013 he went to the Under 19 European Championships where he was named in the top 10 talents after helping Portugal to the semi-finals of the competition.

"I played for Benfica for so long because they are my team – it was my dream. I always wanted to be a football player for Benfica," he says.

He moved to Monaco in 2014 on a season-long loan move, having made three appearances for Benfica's first team – but so impressive were his displays in France, the deal was made permanent just six months into the agreement.

Silva's guile helped Monaco finish third in Ligue 1 and reach the quarter-finals of the Champions League, and having finished third again the following season, Leonardo Jardim's attacking revolution began to gather pace in 2016-17.

Alongside the likes of Radamel Falcao, Fabinho, Benjamin Mendy, Thomas Lemar and Kylian Mbappe, Silva was instrumental in Monaco winning the French title and reaching the Champions League semi-finals, where they beat City en route to the last four. Silva made 51 appearances that season, scoring 10 goals and assisting a further 10, making him one of Europe's most sought-after playmakers.

But it was City who secured his signature. "I'm now at one of the best teams in the world," Bernardo said after signing. "To be part of this club and to have this opportunity is great."

Success immediately followed. He was sensational in his first year as City won the Premier League with a record 100 points and was again instrumental the following season as we won all four domestic trophies for the first time in English football history.

And in 2020-21, his upturn in form halfway through the season was crucial as we won our third Premier League title in four seasons, a fourth successive League Cup and reached the Champions League final.

Ten trophies in four seasons at City, with 35 goals scored in 201 games. Bernardo's impact has been sensational.

EDERSON

"We cannot have a better goalkeeper than Eddie," Pep Guardiola says. "He suits perfectly our way of playing. The impact he has on the team is massive."

Ederson Santana de Moraes joined from Benfica in the summer of 2017, having dislodged Julio Cesar to become the Portuguese side's No. 1. Cesar, a goalkeeper of fine pedigree, had become something of a mentor to Ederson and he was convinced the youngster would be successful if he moved to England. Those words were ringing in his ears when the call came from Guardiola offering him a move to City.

His impact was swift and seismic. More than comfortable with the ball at his feet and possessing an extraordinary range of passing, he has changed the way City play and been central to our period of Premier League supremacy. In his four seasons at the Etihad, the club has won three Premier League titles and reached its first Champions League final.

Guardiola's system requires a goalkeeper comfortable in possession, one who can augment his side's possession-based football. At Barcelona, he had Victor Valdes, while at Bayern Munich it was the original 'sweeper-keeper' Manuel Neuer. Ederson, he feels, is the best passer of them all. "With his feet, he is the best," Guardiola says. "The quality of the pass is the best."

His 60-yard precision passing has become a significant weapon in City's

"I don't practise it that much, maybe two or three times a week. It's a natural skill that I have, to hit long balls, so I don't need to practise it every day"

arsenal. We can go from our own area to a goalscoring position in the final third in the blink of an eye. "I don't practise it that much, maybe two or three times a week," he says. "It's a natural skill that I have, to hit long balls, so I don't need to practise it every day."

He is City's playmaker in goal.

Having played outfield during his youth days back in Brazil – and often playing in midfield during his time at Benfica's academy – it's likely he could do a job in that position for City if needed. Few who have seen his outstanding technique would doubt it.

But it isn't just his ability to be City's 11th outfield player that makes him so valuable – he is also a fine shot stopper.

He collected the Premier League Golden Glove award at the end of the 2019-20 season having kept 16 clean sheets, and then retained the trophy the following year after managing 18 shut-outs. He's the perfect modern-day 'keeper.

Ederson, still only 27, is the latest addition to the pantheon of great Manchester City goalkeepers. He could go on to be the very best.

KYLE WALKER

Pep Guardiola's system has many requirements. He is perhaps the most demanding manager on the planet, with his high-intensity, possession-based style both physically and mentally challenging for his players.

It's particularly difficult for full-backs, who are asked to defend, provide width on the overlap going forward and sometimes step into central-midfield to supplement our numbers in the area of the pitch Guardiola sees as most important. It requires both natural ability and tactical intelligence to truly excel.

There are very few who can cope with the demands, let alone thrive, but Kyle Walker has undoubtedly been one of Europe's best right-backs since swapping Tottenham for Manchester City in 2017, becoming one of Guardiola's most trusted players in the process.

It wasn't an easy task for Walker to adapt at City. Not only did he have the physical and tactical demands Guardiola places on his full-backs to contend with, he was replacing Pablo Zabaleta, a bona fide club legend who occupied a special place in the hearts of City fans.

"How Pep wants to play is unheard of in England," Walker explains. "You don't train for that growing up."

He started off as a forward, and even played at Lilleshall in that position, but unable to get regular starts, he switched to right-back during his time in Sheffield United's academy and never looked back. Walker was given his first start in that role at Under-18s level against Nottingham Forest as a 16-year-old and impressed. "The Nottingham Forest left-winger never beat him once," recalls Ron Reid, his coach at the time. "It was incredible. We gave him another go there the following week and that's how it happened."

Walker has made 496 professional appearances, 184 of those have been for City. He's a vital component of Guardiola's side, both a reliable and explosive element of our game.

"Kyle Walker is brilliant," former City defender and now acclaimed pundit Micah Richards says. "He is one of the most consistent performers I have seen for a long time. I think he has been amazing. Zabaleta and I got a lot of love because he was a warrior and I came through the Academy, but if you actually look at what Kyle's done since he's been here, it's way more than me and Zaba."

Indeed, Walker's style has helped revolutionise City's play. His stamina, pace, desire and technical quality all combine to bring a dimension to City's play few teams can match. With his speed and sheer running power, he basically does the job of two players.

"I try and use my pace in the best way for the team, so we can utilise other people's strengths," Walker says. "If I can let my winger or my attacking midfielder do less defending, then that is my job and if my pace allows me to do that, then brilliant."

"I think Kyle almost changed the way City played," former City captain Richard Dunne explains. "It gave them an opportunity to play more counter-attacking football because he gets forward and back as quick as anything."

Guardiola puts it more simply. "It was an incredible signing for City," he says. "I want to thank the club for bringing him here."

Walker joined City to win trophies and become one of the best full-backs in the game. He's achieved both aims, winning three Premier League titles, one FA Cup and four League Cups, a beacon of consistency throughout. His role is arguably the most demanding, but it also makes him crucial. City's success under Guardiola would not have been possible without him.

Chelsea 0-1 City

WIN AGAINST CHAMPIONS CHANGES MINDSET

30 September 2017

I**t was City's first major test of the 2017-18 season.**

We went into the game away at Stamford Bridge top of the table after taking 16 points from a possible 18, scoring 21 goals in the process, but Chelsea were the defending champions who had beaten City twice en route to their title the previous campaign.

The 3-1 defeat at the Etihad had been particularly chastening for City, who had dominated the early stages and should have gone 2-0 up when Kevin De Bruyne hit the bar from close range. It proved a pivotal moment. City went on to be ruthlessly unpicked by Chelsea's quality in attack and were well beaten. The aftermath had seen us criticised, with Pep Guardiola's philosophy under intense scrutiny.

But the mood in the camp heading into this one was superb. We were top of the league after six games and winning plaudits for the expressive, expansive football we were producing. We had beaten Shakhtar Donetsk in the Champions League four days earlier, and the training sessions since then had been positive. Guardiola and his staff were pleased with the level and there was growing belief among the squad we could challenge for the title, but an injury to Sergio Aguero was a cruel blow.

On Friday morning, the team gathered for breakfast at the CFA, before a 10-minute briefing ahead of an 11am training session used by Guardiola to go through the finer tactical elements of the game that lay ahead. The players had lunch together before retiring to the hotel rooms at the City Football Academy to rest.

At 3.25pm, they departed the CFA and headed to Piccadilly station, where a train carrying the players, management, backroom team and support staff would depart at 3.55pm. Everything ran like clockwork, continuing the smooth preparations that had defined the previous few days.

The atmosphere was relaxed, with most players sat in quiet contemplation of a vitally important game. There was a collective understanding this was a significant fixture; an opportunity to send a message to our rivals that our early-season form would not wane in the same way it had done 12 months earlier. City under Guardiola were now the real deal, and it was time to really lay a marker down.

At 6.50pm, the team checked into the Royal Garden Hotel on Kensington High Street. They had enough time to unpack, before gathering for a team meeting at 7.30pm. Guardiola and his staff went through some set piece routines, an area where they felt

City could have some joy. In games against your rivals, where the margins are so slender, any advantage is welcome, and Guardiola, aided chiefly by his then assistant coach Mikel Arteta, had developed some ideas of how we could exploit Chelsea's backline from corners and free-kicks.

Dinner was served at 8pm, with City's first-team chefs supplying a range of options. There was a salad bar, omelette station, chargrilled chicken, miso salmon, pan fried turbot and grilled calamari, as well as grains, pulses, pasta and a wide selection of vegetables. The appointment of nutritionist Silvia Tremoleda, who had worked with Guardiola at Barcelona, earlier in the year had underlined the importance the City boss places on diet. What goes into the players' bodies fuels their matchday performance and no risks are taken. It's all part of Guardiola's meticulous preparation.

The players spent the remainder of the evening together watching Girona, a fellow City Football Group club, play Celta Vigo in La Liga. It was a frantic 3-3 draw in which the pendulum swung numerous times. Hopefully, some of the players joked, the game tomorrow would be a less stressful affair.

Breakfast was served between 9.30-10am the following morning, and afterwards the players had four hours of downtime. The 5.30pm kick-off may give fans

extra time for their pre-match rituals, but for the players it's a difficult schedule that allows more opportunity for tension to build. Club staff say the key to these matches is minimising nerves and giving the squad every opportunity to relax.

Lunch was served at 2pm, before a final team briefing at the hotel. The message from the backroom staff was clear: the preparation over the previous three days had been close to perfect; now was the time to produce on the pitch.

The team left the hotel and made the short journey to the stadium, arriving 75 minutes before kick-off. Guardiola, unlike his predecessor, Manuel Pellegrini, likes to reach the

ground as late as possible in order to minimise the time the players are waiting. A quick change, warm-ups and then back to the dressing room for a final team talk and then it's game time.

For Chelsea, Eden Hazard, their major creative force and one of the Premier League's finest individual players, was fit again having missed the opening weeks of the campaign. It was a huge boost for the champions. He is a player so difficult to stop, lightening quick on the ball and able to beat players with ease.

But City were imperious.

We dominated the game from start to finish, the 1-0 scoreline flattering the

home side. City may not have created as many clear-cut chances as we would have liked, but it was us who dictated play. It would be difficult to find a more one-sided game between two of the Premier League's proverbial 'Top Six,' and our place at the top of the table was maintained.

The winning goal, scored by De Bruyne, was a moment of pure brilliance. Gabriel Jesus laid the ball back into his path and, 20 yards out, he took one touch with his right before unleashing an unstoppable drive with his weaker left into the top corner past Thibaut Courtois.

The frenzied celebrations in the corner in front of the travelling City fans spoke volumes.

"We are so happy," Guardiola said afterwards. "The most important thing is to win the game but the way we played, especially in the second half, was pleasing.

"We had control and in the second half we adjusted our possession and the way we attacked. They could not play and had to do long balls."

In the dressing room after the game, the players were jubilant. Some sat staring in delight, others cheered and sang. The statement they had so badly wanted to make had

been emphatically delivered. This side had title-winning qualities.

Once the dressing-room celebrations died down, the team boarded the coach and headed for Luton airport in buoyant mood. Traffic on the roads delayed their journey, but nothing could dampen the spirits. The players were singing, joking and laughing throughout. Belief was visibly growing.

"That, I think, was the first day we believe in ourselves, me included, to say, okay, we can go away on the biggest stage and win," Guardiola said during a mid-season break in Abu Dhabi the following year. "The season before, the games against the big contenders....the results were poor.

"The way we played against Chelsea, we could have won 2-0 or 3-0. That was so important for all of us. We knew now we were able to go away and make a good performance."

There were many significant moments on the way to our record-breaking title win that saw us collect 100 points and redefine what it means to win the Premier League comfortably. But it was arguably this day that had the most significant effect on the squad's collective belief.

Napoli 2-4 City

SERGIO STRIKES IN ITALY TO BECOME CLUB'S ALL-TIME LEADING GOALSCORER

1 November 2017

City's trip to the Stadio San Paolo was, by any measure, a mouth-watering fixture.

Both sides were unbeaten in their respective leagues, with City top of the Premier League having won nine and drawn one of our opening 10 matches, while Maurizio Sarri's Napoli were at the summit of Serie A, with just two points dropped from their opening 11 games.

And not only were the two sides winning machines, they were playing with beauty and freedom, too. With managers committed to attacking football, they had plundered 67 league goals between them in their combined 21 matches thus far.

It was a game between Europe's two most free-flowing sides.

The occasion did not disappoint. In a game that ebbed and flowed, City were outplayed in the opening period but came from behind to win 4-2 and seal qualification for the knock-out phase by making it 12 points from 12 in Group F. The result extended our unbeaten run to 22 games in all competitions, our best ever sequence without defeat.

But the night took on added significance when Sergio Aguero scored to put us 3-2 up with 20 minutes remaining.

It was the striker's 178th goal in a City shirt, meaning he surpassed Eric Brook's 78-year record to become the club's all-time leading goalscorer. His name was already etched in City folklore with his goal against QPR in 2012 that sealed our first league title in 44 years, but

this rubber stamped his place in the pantheon of City greats.

The speed with which Aguero had reached 178 was remarkable. Brook's 177 came in 494 appearances. Aguero had surpassed him having played 264 times, a record that further underlined his world-class ability in the final third.

"When one guy achieves what he has achieved, there's big congratulations," Pep Guardiola said afterwards. "He's a legend for the club, for the history, and everybody has to be so proud of that."

It was a fitting arena for Aguero to notch up a major milestone; the spiritual home of Diego Maradona in the city he remains such an iconic figure. Aguero was once married to Maradona's daughter

Giannina – she is the mother of his son Benjamin – and he had played under Maradona at international level, most notably at the 2010 World Cup.

"I am very happy – this moment is once in a lifetime!" Aguero said after the game.

"This [shirt] is for my son. He texted me to say: if I score, to bring the shirt to him! I am happy because the team helped support me with the City fans and the staff.

"Thank you very much everyone. Now, I am enjoying this moment."

No one would begrudge Aguero those celebrations. Recognised across the world as one of the finest strikers to have played the game, he was now officially the highest scoring Manchester City player of all time.

Gracias, Kun!

City 2-1 Southampton

LATE STERLING WINNER SEALS CLUB-RECORD 12TH SUCCESSIVE PREMIER LEAGUE VICTORY

29 November 2017

If there's a moment that **illustrated what an outstanding match-winner Raheem Sterling had become under the guidance of Pep Guardiola, perhaps this was it.**

Southampton were the visitors in late November 2017. City knew a win would seal a club-record 12th successive Premier League victory and restore our eight-point lead over Manchester United at the top of the table.

We took the lead two minutes into the second-half through Kevin De Bruyne, who whipped a fine free-kick past Saints 'keeper Fraser Forster at the near post.

It was a moment of ingenuity and yet another example of his productivity. Since his Premier League debut in September 2015, the Belgian had directly contributed to 51 goals in the competition (17 goals, 34 assists), more than any other midfielder during that time.

City were dominant thereafter, but with 15 minutes remaining, Oriol Romeu levelled for Southampton,

lashing home first time off the underside of the bar after Sofiane Boufal's cutback.

It had been a frustrating night, with City's profligacy and a string of fine Forster saves keeping the score level. Going into the final few seconds, City had enjoyed 75 percent possession and had 25 shots (12 on target) to the visitors' seven (two on target). Yet this was looking like two points dropped in disappointing fashion.

But in the 96th minute, Sterling, like all top players, produced a moment of pure brilliance to seal a significant three points and spark wild scenes of jubilation, both on the pitch and in the Etihad stands.

He picked the ball up on the left wing and began to cut inside – his trademark move – but there were 10 Southampton players inside the box making his path to goal almost impossible. Sterling instead squared it to De Bruyne on the edge of the area, and four defenders immediately ran towards the ball in an attempt to close him down.

That created two yards of space for Sterling, and when De Bruyne found him with a pass back into his feet, the England forward took a touch with his left foot to set himself before curling a quite magnificent effort into the top corner.

He turned and ran the full length of the pitch in pure celebration, the significance of the moment clear to him and everyone else.

Guardiola and his staff were jubilant; the City fans rejoiced.

Indeed, referee Paul Tierney had to go over and speak to Guardiola in a bid to calm him down before play restarted, with the City boss admitting afterwards he lost control of his emotions.

"I apologised, I could not control it," Guardiola acknowledged. "I was so happy, like all the fans and all the players. I wanted to run behind Ras, but I am not fast enough. We are so happy."

It was the third decisive late goal Sterling had scored in a week after dramatic winners against Feyenoord and Huddersfield, but this one felt the most important. This was proving his most prolific season to date, with the England international having been directly involved in 12 goals in his last 13 competitive appearances (10 goals, two assists).

"Raheem is a match-winner, it was a fantastic goal, I am so happy for him," Guardiola said.

"As I have said many times, he is making steps. Before he was a little bit more shy and he did not believe, but now he can do that.

"I think his team-mates give him the confidence and say, 'we trust in you' but then you have to have the personality to do what he did in the last minute."

The victory saw City become the first side to reach 40 points from 14 games of a Premier League season, and this felt like a major moment in our bid to win the title.

Manchester United 1-2 City

CITY SET NEW ENGLISH RECORD FOR CONSECUTIVE TOP-FLIGHT WINS

10 December 2017

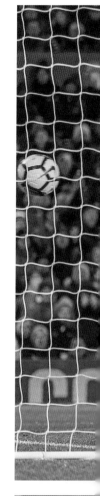

Another Manchester derby at Old Trafford, another memorable win for City.

Pep Guardiola's side went into the game having dropped just two points from our opening 15 games of the season. Our levels of consistency had risen significantly but our opponents were lagging. United, who sat nine points behind in second, were our most serious rivals. This was our toughest fixture so far and people wanted to know if our near-perfect start could be halted.

But City turned on the style and dominated. We won 2-1, a victory that saw us move 11 points clear at the top – an incredible lead to have established after just 16 matches of the season – and, in the process, we became the first team in English football history to win 14 consecutive top-flight matches in a single season. It was only December, but it really did feel as though City were already champions-elect.

David Silva, the best player on the pitch by some distance, opened the scoring when he hooked the ball into the net after hesitation in the United defence, before Marcus Rashford equalised in first-half injury time.

However, Nicolas Otamendi bagged a deserved second-half winner, volleying home a loose ball after Romelu Lukaku's attempted clearance had hit his own player.

The result ended United's 40-match unbeaten home run, a sequence which stretched back 15 months to our win in September 2016. And in a marker of how dominant City were, United posted a 35 percent possession figure, their lowest tally at Old Trafford in the Premier League since 2003-04 (when Opta started collecting such data).

After the game, amid talk of City having an unassailable lead at such an early juncture, Guardiola refused to be drawn on celebrating too soon.

"We are still in December," the City manager cautioned. "If we have an 11-point lead when we play the second derby in April then maybe I will tell you that we have the title.

"We won at Old Trafford again, that is why I am the most pleased and, of course, for the three points," he added. "We played good, with a lot of courage. I'm so satisfied."

United manager Jose Mourinho focused on a 79th-minute incident that saw Ander Herrera booked for diving after going down under a challenge from Otamendi in his post-match analysis.

"My first reaction is I feel sorry for (referee) Michael Oliver because he had a very good match but, unfortunately, he made an important mistake," Mourinho said. "The result was made with a big penalty not given. That would have been 2-2. Michael was unlucky because it was a clear penalty."

But Guardiola wasn't going to have City's win diminished. In his eyes, and those of most observers, City were more than deserved winners.

"Last season it was the same – we won here, and it was the referee. Today as well," he added.

"We are an honest team. We had 65 percent ball possession, which means we wanted to play. We came here and did that. It's not true that my players go down easily. That is not an argument I believe."

AYMERIC LAPORTE

"For me, when he is fit, he is the best left-sided centre-back in the world," manager Pep Guardiola declared in January 2020 when asked about Aymeric Laporte.

Laporte has many qualities. Quick, strong in the air and able to time challenges beautifully, he is a powerful defender who adds muscle to City's backline.

But it is perhaps the accuracy of his left foot that represents his most potent weapon. Laporte can switch play in an instant with a 60-yard pass of remarkable precision. It's rare to see a defender with such extreme technical quality. It became a key feature of City's play immediately after his arrival.

Laporte joined City in January 2018 as a 23-year-old. Arriving from Athletic Bilbao, a side known for their intense passing style, he signed a deal until 2023.

"I am very happy to be here," Laporte declared. "City are a club with a lot of ambition and they are one of the best teams in Europe."

His football journey began in France, playing youth football with hometown club SU Agen, before moving to Bayonne.

His switch to Spanish football saw his senior career ignite. He joined Bilbao in 2012, and after representing their B side and gaining first-team experience with CD Basconia, he forced his way into the first-team setup.

In total, he clocked up 222 appearances for the Spanish side, scoring ten goals.

Capable of playing as a left-back, Laporte was named in La Liga's 2013/14 Team of the Year. In the 2015/16 campaign, he helped Athletic Bilbao to Supercopa de Espana glory

– their first piece of major silverware for 31 years.

He adapted to life at City with ease and immediately impressed. By the end of the 2018-19 season, he had already become a Premier League champion, playing nine times as City set a new record of 100 points. His arrival in the January had given City a boost, and he looked set to play an even more important role the following season.

And so it proved. He became City's first-choice central-defender as we became the first team in English football history to win all four domestic trophies in a single season. Laporte played 51 games, scoring five goals and providing three assists. He was flawless throughout.

However, his wings were clipped the following season after damaging his cartilage and lateral meniscus during a win over Brighton in August 2019. Laporte travelled to Barcelona for surgery under the watchful eye of Dr Ramon Cugat and began his recovery. He made a tentative return to the side the following January and finished the season with 20 appearances in all competitions.

John Stones' resurgence saw Laporte play less during the 2020-21 season, but he still managed 27 appearances across all competitions. He scored the winner in the League Cup final as City made it four successes in a row, and was a key part of our league title success and run to the Champions League final.

Laporte's impact in three-and-a-half years at City has been emphatic: 111 games, eight goals and seven trophies.

And at 27, his best years still lie ahead. His future is incredibly bright.

City 5-1 Leicester

KUN SCORES FOUR TO REAFFIRM HIS WORLD-CLASS STATUS

10 February 2018

Further proof, as if it were needed, of Sergio Aguero's world-class finishing ability was provided at the Etihad Stadium as the Argentine scored four goals in City's 5-1 victory over Leicester.

In a remarkable display of his ruthless goalscoring qualities, it was the third time Aguero had scored four or more goals in a single Premier League match, more than any other player in the competition's history.

Raheem Sterling struck the opener after three minutes, tapping home at the back post after an outrageous first-time pass from Kevin De Bruyne.

But Jamie Vardy, so often the scourge of our backline, capitalised on a misplaced pass from Nicolas Otamendi and equalised after 24 minutes to see the sides go in at half-time level.

The second-half, however, was an Aguero masterclass as City won comfortably.

He restored our lead just after the break, tapping home from close range after another inch-perfect De Bruyne ball across the box, and that same pairing combined for City's third as Aguero powered the ball past Foxes 'keeper Kasper Schmeichel.

It meant a hat-trick of assists for De Bruyne, reaffirming once more his outstanding ability to find a perfectly-weighted pass in the final third.

It was also his 14th assist of the Premier League season so far, four more than teammate Leroy Sané,

his nearest challenger in the assist stakes.

Aguero then completed his hat-trick by pouncing on Schmeichel's misplaced pass before impudently chipping the Leicester 'keeper. It was a moment of brilliance and audacity, further illustrating his supreme confidence in front of goal.

And his fourth was arguably the best of the lot. As he collected Phil Foden's pass outside the area, there was seemingly little danger for Leicester, but this, after all, was Aguero. He took a touch to steady himself and another to get the ball out from under his feet and then produced an incredible 20-yard drive that cannoned in off the crossbar. Remarkable.

His quartet meant Aguero had scored in seven consecutive games at the Etihad Stadium in all competitions (14 goals) for the first

time in his illustrious Manchester City career, including two hat-tricks in three games. It also took his tally of Premier League goals for the season to 21, meaning he became only the fourth player to score 20 plus goals in four consecutive campaigns - after Alan Shearer, Thierry Henry (five) and Harry Kane.

The result moved City 16 points clear at the top of the Premier League table. It left us needing a maximum 21 points from our final 11 games of the season to secure our third league title in six years.

"My advice for the players is not to think how many games are left, just to look to the next one," City manager Pep Guardiola said afterwards. "If we are able to win the title it will be something special."

City, it seemed, had moved into cruise control.

CARABAO CUP FINAL 2018
WINNERS

Arsenal 0-3 City

KOMPANY DAZZLES AT WEMBLEY AS GUARDIOLA LANDS MAIDEN CITY TROPHY

25 February 2018

City's first season under Pep Guardiola was one of transition. The squad left behind by Manuel Pellegrini needed refreshing if it was to become capable of realising Guardiola's demands, while the Catalan's ideas needed time to embed.

By his second season at the Etihad helm, however, City had been revolutionised. Flying in the Premier League and on course for a significant points tally, the League Cup final in February 2018 provided an opportunity for Guardiola to win his first piece of silverware in English football and for the squad to lay down a springboard for further success.

We faced Arsenal, 27 points behind us in the Premier League, but a side packed full of quality and experience. Given we had exited the FA Cup six days earlier at the hands of Wigan Athletic, ending hopes of an unprecedented Quadruple, this would be a test of City's mettle as much as our ability.

But City were imperious. Arsenal, a team loaded with international footballers, simply couldn't live with us. We won 3-0 but it could easily have been more.

Sergio Aguero nudged Shkodran Mustafi aside easily before lobbing David Ospina from just outside the area to give City an 18th-minute lead with his 30th goal of the season in all competitions.

Just like in the 2016 League Cup final against Liverpool, Vincent Kompany was the man of the match. His performance that day was exceptional, but this one against Arsenal dwarfed it.

The skipper was a colossus.

Appropriately enough, it was the Belgian who scored City's second, turning Ilkay Gundogan's cross-cum-shot into the net from close range.

David Silva wrapped the victory up on 65 minutes, rolling Callum Chambers inside the area before finishing superbly.

Even Arsenal manager Arsene Wenger had to admit there was little his side could do on a day City produced their best on the big stage. "When you lose a game like that everything is questioned," Wenger said. "But we played against a good side, you cannot say that we played against an average side. They dominate the Premier League, and they have good players. It is difficult to come back."

This was Wenger's third defeat in a League Cup final, a competition he hadn't managed to win during his 21 years as Arsenal boss.

Guardiola was delighted – but he insisted the win was not about his own personal record, rather it was for Manchester City as a whole.

"This win is not for me, it's for Manchester City," the manager pointed out.

"The first half was not good – too many mistakes with simple passes – but the second half we played with more courage, more personality. That is why we were outstanding after the break.

"It was so important we won this after going out of the FA Cup. Now we have to focus absolutely on the Premier League and trying to win the games we need to win the title and try and progress to the Champions League quarter-final."

City 3-1 Brighton

CITY CLOSE IN ON UNPRECEDENTED CENTURY AS YAYA BIDS FAREWELL

9 May 2018

City registered a hat-trick of significant Premier League milestones thanks to a 3-1 win over Brighton at the Etihad in our penultimate game of the 2017/18 campaign.

The result moved City on to 97 points – a record Premier League haul – leaving one game left for us to chalk up a perfect 100.

It also meant we had set a record for the largest number of wins in a Premier League season, with our tally of 31 surpassing the 30 registered by Chelsea the previous year and equalled the all-time top-flight record set by Tottenham's double-winning team of 1960-61.

And City had now plundered 105 goals, another Premier League milestone, eclipsing the 103 Chelsea managed in 2009-10.

There could be no doubt Pep Guardiola's outstanding team were going down in history.

"They are, I think, the best footballing side that I have seen, certainly in the Premier League," was Brighton manager Chris Hughton's succinct post-match analysis. It was becoming increasingly difficult to argue with his assertion.

Leroy Sané created all three of City's goals, becoming the first player to register three assists in a single game that season; Danilo, Bernardo Silva and Fernandinho were the scorers.

With records tumbling, it was clear this was a City side further raising the bar and redefining Premier League standards, but in true Guardiola fashion, he challenged his players to deliver more.

"We cannot deny, we are so proud of the records," the manager said. "I am not saying we are the best [Premier League side ever] but we did the best season ever. Nobody scored more goals, more points. Now it's 97 so if someone wants to beat that record, they have to be good and win a lot of games. Today is a special day.

"To be considered one of the best, you have to win more. To be alongside United in the 1990s or Liverpool in the 1980s you have to win more.

"I am not saying we are a legend team, I am not saying we are better than them. No, because you have to make more years to do that, but in one season we were better than all of them in the history of the Premier League and the history of English football."

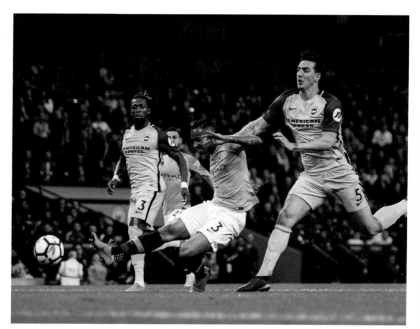

The night was also an emotional one, as City fans said goodbye to Yaya Touré, a remarkable midfielder who had served the club with distinction during an eight-year period.

Touré scored 81 goals in 316 games and delivered countless magical moments, winning three Premier League titles, an FA Cup and three League Cups along the way.

His brother Kolo, who played for City between 2009-13, was brought on to the Etihad pitch after the game to present Yaya with a commemorative City shirt.

"He will always be part of the club and will be loved," Guardiola said. "His speech afterwards in the changing room was absolutely amazing."

One more game and a shot at an incredible century of Premier League points beckoned. This was becoming a dream season no City fan would ever forget.

Southampton 0-1 City
JESUS WINNER SECURES RECORD-BREAKING 100 POINTS
13 May 2018

Most people thought it would never happen. There are only 114 points available each Premier League season. To reach treble figures in a single campaign surely requires a consistency a division of this strength makes impossible. This, after all, is the hardest league in the world, with a depth of quality that means easy games are a rarity.

But City under Pep Guardiola were reaching new heights, playing football at a level we'd never seen on these shores and, guided by his principles and ideas, his side managed to achieve the impossible.

And how fitting that after such an astonishing season it ended in a flourish, with Gabriel Jesus' late, late goal securing a final-day 1-0 win over Southampton and ensuring the 100-point landmark was reached in thrilling and spectacular fashion.

With the drama and excitement came a new addition to the list of incredibly important late goals in City's history. Jesus' beautiful lob seconds before the final whistle now stands proudly alongside Paul Dickov's strike at Wembley in '99 and Sergio Aguero's 2012 title-clinching winner. Typical City, ever the entertainers.

It confirmed City's 32nd win of the campaign. 50 points earned at home; 50 points earned away. A Premier League record 19-point winning margin. Just two defeats. An extraordinary, record-breaking season few could have predicted.

Guardiola's celebration when Jesus scored our 106th Premier League goal of the season told its own story. His emotions spilled over, the enormity of what he and his squad had achieved not lost on him, even in the heat of the moment. Jesus, the hero of the hour, immediately ran to the away end to celebrate with the delirious travelling fans. Kyle Walker, without socks or boots, led the charge from the bench. Fernandinho's flip flops went home with a supporter, a wonderfully weird souvenir of a crazy day. This is what football is all about.

"A lot of goals scored, few conceded, lots of points, wins at home, wins away, everything was perfect this season – and we finished the way we deserved to finish," Guardiola said afterwards. "Premier League, 100 points, I still cannot believe it – it is a massive achievement."

In truth, City's performance at St Mary's was way below the standard we'd set during the season. We appeared somewhat nervous, the looming milestone and immortalisation that would come if we achieved it weighing heavy on the players. Kevin De Bruyne was the man of the match, and it was fitting his beautiful pass that assisted Jesus saw him clock up his 16th assist of the campaign, meaning he won the inaugural Playmaker of the Season award.

On a perfect day for City, teenagers Phil Foden and Brahim Dias were introduced as late substitutes, ensuring they clocked up five appearances for the season and each received one of the 40 Premier League medals handed to the squad.

"One hundred points is a lot, 50 points at home, 50 points away, it means how stable, how good we were all the season," Guardiola said in the aftermath. "The numbers are always consequences of what we have done in terms of the way we play, our mentality. You cannot achieve what we achieve in terms of many, many records if you are not a humble team, professional, [that] has that desire to take the ball and win and win and win."

Indeed, the list of Premier League records City had broken during the campaign was sensational. Most points, most consecutive Premier League victories, biggest winning margin, most consecutive away wins, biggest share of away possession, fewest minutes trailing, quickest to a century of goals and best goal difference. By pretty much every conceivable metric, it was total domination.

"After we won the Premier League, we wanted to keep motivated, to keep winning games," Bernardo Silva said after the game. "To reach 100 points for the first time in Premier League history is fantastic and we are so happy."

During his first season in charge, which had seen City undergo a transitional process, the English media had questioned Guardiola's methods. Could his possession-based football work in the Premier League? Was the English game simply too robust for his ideas to take hold?

His answer was emphatic. City blew the opposition away over the course of a remarkable season, setting new records and raising standards along the way.

"It must be an absolute joy to be a Manchester City fan and watch that football," Premier League legend Alan Shearer said on BBC Match of the Day that night. He wasn't wrong.

The team were christened the Centurions; their place in the history books assured. Statistically, the greatest in Premier League history. It was a special season for everyone connected to Manchester City Football Club.

CENTURIONS

EARLIEST TITLE WIN

City's claiming of the title with five matches to go equals the record that was set by Manchester United in 2000/01.

BIGGEST WINNING MARGIN

City finished 19 points clear of Man Utd, whose record we have broken. United ended 18 points clear at the top in 1999/00.

MOST CONSECUTIVE PREMIER LEAGUE VICTORIES

The 18-match winning run that City enjoyed between victory at AFC Bournemouth on 26 August and the 1-0 win at Newcastle United on 27 December broke two records: the record of 13 consecutive wins in the same campaign, held jointly by Arsenal (2001/02) and Chelsea (2016/17); and Arsenal's overall record of 14 consecutive league victories, achieved between February and August 2002.

MOST CONSECUTIVE AWAY WINS

The victory at Newcastle was City's 11th away win in a row, a sequence that started on 21 May last season. That matched the record set by Chelsea between 6 April 2008 and 7 December 2008.

BIGGEST SHARE OF AWAY POSSESSION

City had 82.13 per cent of possession at Everton on 31 March, the highest by an away team in a Premier League match since these records began.

MOST OPPONENTS BEATEN

City have beaten all the other 19 Premier League teams this season, becoming only the third side to do so after Manchester United, in 2010/11, and Chelsea, in 2005/06.

FEWEST MINUTES TRAILED

City were behind in matches for a total of only 153 minutes, the fewest by a side in a single campaign.

MOST SUCCESSIVE MANAGER OF THE MONTH AWARDS

Guardiola was named Barclays Manager of the Month four times in a row between September and December, which is a first.

QUICKEST TO A CENTURY

With their four goals against West Ham United, City recorded 102 goals in 35 matches, the quickest a Premier League side has reached a century of goals in a single campaign. It is the fourth time 100 goals has been scored in a Premier League season, following Chelsea in 2009/10 and City and Liverpool in 2013/14.

MOST POINTS

City are the only team in English top-flight history to reach 100 points in a single season. They reached that century with a stoppage-time winner at Southampton, which came after they beat Brighton & Hove Albion in their previous match to break Chelsea's record of 95 points set from 2004/05.

MOST AWAY POINTS

With the final-day win over Southampton, City also surpassed Chelsea's 48 away points picked up in 2004/05. Pep Guardiola's side finished on 50 points on their travels.

MOST TOTAL WINS

That victory over Saints was City's 32nd of the campaign, moving us further ahead of the mark of 30 recorded by Chelsea last season. City are the first team to win 32 matches in a single English top-flight season.

MOST AWAY WINS

Jose Mourinho's Chelsea of 2004/05 won 15 matches away from home, another feat that City surpassed on the final day with their 16th away victory.

MOST GOALS

City scored 106 goals, beating that of Chelsea's 103 scored in the 2009/10 campaign.

BEST GOAL DIFFERENCE

City's goal difference of +79 is eight better than the previous best set by the Chelsea team of 2009/10 who finished with +71.

RIYAD MAHREZ

Manchester City's dominance under Pep Guardiola has brought new challenges, most notably the tendency for opposition sides to defend in numbers in order to make life difficult for us to attack with freedom. When teams put men behind the ball and make it hard for us to weave intricate passing moves, it requires someone who can create space by beating players, providing a moment of magic to unlock the door. Few players in the game do that quite as well as Riyad Mahrez.

"He has a special quality," Pep Guardiola says. "He is a guy who dances on the pitch. He doesn't lose balls. He attracts opponents on the pitch and after he makes a pass in behind."

He joined City in 2018 from Leicester, where he'd played a key role in The Foxes' fairy-tale 2015-16 Premier League title success, one of sport's most unlikely triumphs. In their win at the Etihad in February of that season, seen as a pivotal moment that ratcheted up Leicester's belief they could win the league, Mahrez was outstanding, assisting their opener and scoring a brilliant second in a 3-1 win. He ended that season by winning the PFA Player of the Year award, widely seen as the ultimate individual prize in the English game, with his stock rising rapidly.

Two years later and City secured his signature, with Guardiola, a manager who never stands still, craving an added dimension to our play after the 2017-18 Centurions campaign.

"Watching City from afar has been a pleasure," Mahrez said upon signing for the club. And so began a successful partnership. His first season saw the winger play 44 times (scoring 12 and assisting 12) as City won the Premier League, FA Cup and League

Cup – the first team ever to achieve the feat. His goal at Brighton on the final day, as we came from behind to win 4-1 and seal the title with 98 points, was a beautiful moment in a wonderful campaign.

But it was perhaps the 2020-21 season that represents his most influential in a City shirt. He played 48 times as City won the Premier

> "He has a special quality. He is a guy who dances on the pitch. He doesn't lose balls"

League and League Cup and reached our first-ever Champions League final. In the semi-final against Paris Saint-Germain, Mahrez was the star of the two legs, scoring the winner in a 2-1 first-leg victory in France, before bagging a double at home to seal a 4-1 aggregate success.

His successes and statistics tell their own story, but there's an aesthetic beauty to Mahrez's play. He has the best first touch in the City squad (watching him kill a ball is often a thing of beauty) and he possesses unrivalled close control.

And it isn't just in Manchester where he is idolised. Mahrez has a fervent following across Africa, particularly in Algeria, his father's country of birth. Mahrez led Algeria to their second Africa Cup of Nation success in 2019, capping a remarkable year that had seen him reach the summit of the English game by helping City win a clean-sweep of domestic trophies.

In his three years at City, he has won seven trophies, playing 142 games and scoring 39.

Mahrez provides City with an edge. There's no one quite like him in our ranks.

Chelsea 0-2 City

AGUERO REACHES 200 CITY GOALS TO SECURE COMMUNITY SHIELD VICTORY

5 August 2018

Manchester City lifted the 2018 Community Shield with a convincing Wembley win over Chelsea.

Sergio Aguero grabbed the headlines, scoring twice in a man-of-the-match display that saw him move past 200 goals for the club.

The striker had become City's all-time top scorer when he bagged the third in a Champions League 4-2 win over Napoli in November 2017 as he edged past Eric Brook's 78-year record. Brook managed 177 for City, but Aguero was now moving comfortably clear at the top of the charts and continually rewriting the club's history books.

It took just 13 minutes for Aguero to open his 2018-19 account for the season. He collected the ball on the edge of the area after Phil Foden surged forward and fired low into the bottom corner past former City 'keeper Willy Caballero. It was a fine strike that brought up his City double century.

And just before the hour mark, the Argentine master marksman made it 201, with another fine finish having gathered Bernardo Silva's pass.

Those two goals meant 10 of Aguero's 201 strikes in all competitions for City had come against Chelsea – only against Newcastle (14) had he scored more – and his five Wembley goals is more than any other player in our history.

Having hit such a significant milestone, this was Aguero's day – but the performance of Foden in City's midfield also made everyone take note.

In scorching conditions, Foden delivered an effortless display. He was at the centre of everything City did well going forward, with his exceptional movement, passing and vision all in abundant evidence.

The performances he had delivered for City's Academy teams since joining as a nine-year-old had every City fan excited – but promise and expectation was now being fulfilled on the senior stage. City clearly had a star in the making, with his performance against Chelsea offering an exciting glimpse into the future.

"He was ready last season. Now he is one year on, he is more mature," manager Pep Guardiola said afterwards.

"He was training last season with us, and he fought well with all of our players. It is so good to have another player with his talent. He's a City fan – and Mancunian – and it is so good for us."

Indeed, Foden would become a first-team regular throughout the 2018-19 campaign, with his improved physical condition allowing him to compete at the highest level on a regular basis.

For City, the Community Shield provided a launchpad for what would be the club's greatest-ever season – the first of an incredible four-trophy haul no other side had managed in the history of English football.

City 2-1 Liverpool
CHAMPIONS RECLAIM GROUND IN TENSE TITLE RACE
3 January 2019

It was the night City's 2018/19 title challenge was reignited in spectacular fashion.

After our 100-point record haul the previous season, Liverpool, galvanised by the management of Jurgen Klopp and an influx of impressive new players, had returned stronger than ever. By the turn of the year, they remained unbeaten and had established a seven-point lead that their form suggested was close to unassailable.

If City were going to become the first side in a decade to win back-to-back Premier League titles, victory in this match felt imperative. Defeat would open up a 10-point gap, a surely insurmountable deficit, even for this City side.

"Winning felt vital, but Liverpool were unbeaten all season and looked like they were never going to lose a game ever again," recalls Mike Hammond, a City season ticket holder.

"We simply had to win. It had felt like the game had been on the horizon for weeks. It had ruined Christmas because it was always there in the back of your mind. It was win or bust."

It was by no means a classic, but City came out on top, winning 2-1 and closing the gap on Liverpool to four points. These were arguably the two best teams in Europe, but the magnitude of the occasion meant it was a tense, somewhat fraught affair. Becoming champions requires winning matches in whatever way possible, and City did just that on an unforgettable night at the Etihad that saw the atmosphere reach fever pitch.

"There was incredible tension on the way to the ground and you could feel it when we got inside," Hammond explains. "But they're the nights that bring out the best in the fans. The atmosphere was absolutely electric."

City had almost fallen behind in the first half but for a dramatic goal line clearance from John Stones. Sadio Mane's effort had hit the post, and Stones' initial attempted clearance cannoned off Ederson and rebounded towards goal. Stones, at full stretch, managed to hook the ball clear with millimetres to spare as City survived a major scare.

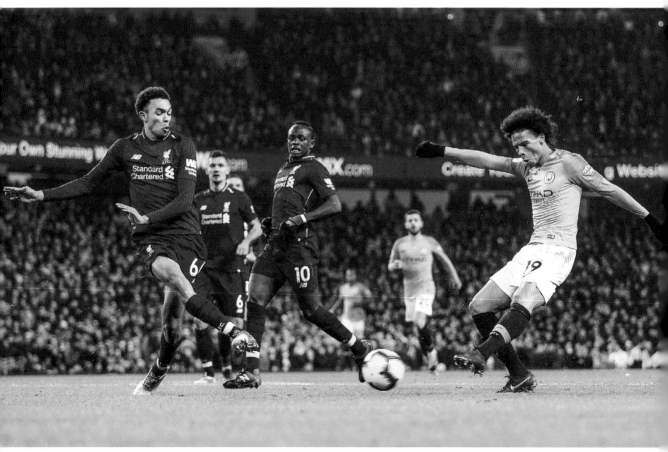

"The Stones clearance was at my end of the ground and from where I was sat it looked over the line," explains Hammond. "Just before that, Vincent Kompany had fouled [Mohamed] Salah and only got a yellow card when it easily could have been red. So, you just felt it might be our night."

Sergio Aguero opened the scoring five minutes before half-time, firing an unstoppable effort from a tight angle past Alisson at the near post. This was archetypal Aguero: the most lethal striker in Premier League history once again demonstrating his frightening efficiency.

"It was pure Sergio," says Hammond. "One of the best goals you would ever want to see. In such a crucial game, there's only him who would do that."

Roberto Firmino headed Liverpool level just after the hour mark, but 18 minutes from time, Leroy Sané struck the winner – perhaps the most important contribution of his City career – firing in off the post with expert precision to finish off a swift counter that began with Ederson intercepting a Liverpool throughball on the edge of his own area.

A nervous finale ensued, but City held on amid deafening noise and palpable tension.

This was turning into a classic title race. Two thoroughbred teams at their very best, redefining what was necessary to be champions of England. The bar had been raised by City the previous campaign and Liverpool had somehow joined the party. This was consistency and quality on a scale the Premier League had never seen before.

"I am proud of them, but not just today," City manager Pep Guardiola said afterwards. "We lost two games in four days, but you can't forget what they have done for 16 months. We knew that it was a final today, if we lose it is almost over.

"All credit to these incredible players. That is how we have to play in the Champions League. Both teams tried to search for each other, we were not scared, we had no fear, and we had a lot of pressure.

"They are leaders - it is four points, but we have reduced the gap. We knew that if we won, we would be in contention to fight for the Premier League, if we lose it is over.

"I don't remember a league so tough, there are so many huge contenders fighting for the title. Every game is a final."

And if anyone still needs an example of what makes Bernardo Silva such a special player, they should watch this game for definitive evidence.

The midfielder's technical proficiency is obvious – he has quick feet, can produce skill in tight areas and has an eye for a pass – but the humility and selflessness with which he plays is what separates him from so many others. In this game, a crucial, must-win occasion, he ran a remarkable 13.7km, giving everything to ensure City came away with three points against our fiercest Premier League title rival.

This was Bernardo in a nutshell: a brilliant technician and one of the most altruistic players in the game.

For City to win the title this year, against such a strong opponent, it was going to require a near-perfect final five months of the season. Liverpool remained in pole position, but this result meant the race was very much back on.

City 6-0 Chelsea

BEAUTIFUL FOOTBALL TOO MUCH FOR CHELSEA

10 February 2019

Beautiful football. It's a phrase that has become synonymous with Manchester City, particularly under the management of Pep Guardiola. It's one used to describe our aesthetic: the bewitching possession-based approach; the electric pace of our play; the improvised, skilful brilliance; the non-stop thirst for goals.

"If you have the ball as much as possible then the opponent does not have the ball," Guardiola says in typically simple fashion. "Maybe one day they will change the rules but I think to score a goal you need the ball."

But City's style can also be characterised by hard work. There are no passengers. Every player is expected to run without the ball, pressing high and hard in a bid to regain possession as quickly as possible after losing it. Guardiola has designed training ground drills to encourage exactly that, and if players fall below his expectations they are soon taken out of the side.

"Off the ball, they have to run like it was the last minute of their life," he says. "I don't like it when I see a player who doesn't run. I don't like it at all.

"They have to convince me why the other teammates can run and this guy cannot run. If he convinces me of that and convinces his mates, maybe. If he doesn't run for the other ones I don't understand the theory."

When both the artistry and industry come together, it's mesmerising.

There have been plenty of matches that typify beautiful football in the last 10 years, one of which is the 6-0 win over Chelsea at the Etihad Stadium in February 2019, a performance showcasing everything that makes City so special.

We were 4-0 up after a breath-taking opening 25 minutes that left Chelsea shellshocked. Raheem Sterling set us on our way, Sergio Aguero scored twice in six minutes and Ilkay Gundogan added a fourth. It was high-intensity, pass-and-move football with a ruthless edge.

Aguero completed his hat-trick in the second half, for what was his 11th Premier League treble. It moved him joint-top of the list of all-time Premier League hat-tricks alongside the great Alan Shearer.

Sterling added another with 10 minutes remaining to underline City's total dominance on a wonderful day at the Etihad that saw the side return to the top of the Premier League table.

"To score six against Chelsea and the way we played, we had so much attention," Guardiola said after watching his side come close to perfection. "We did it, it's an incredible compliment to the players, they are outstanding.

"We spoke this morning, we trained set pieces, trained some movements and I never thought we would score this amount of goals."

"The goal after three minutes made it very difficult to play against these opponents," admitted shell-shocked Chelsea manager Maurizio Sarri. "They played fantastic football."

The result saw City become the first top-flight team since Tottenham Hotspur in December 1965 to score more than once in 15 consecutive home league matches.

City don't always scale the heady heights of this game – it would be unreasonable to expect them to – but this way of playing is what Guardiola works every single day to try and achieve. Chelsea, a side full of world-class international players, were beaten into submission by City's bewitching blend of flair, skill and sheer hard work.

It was the epitome of the beautiful football paradigm.

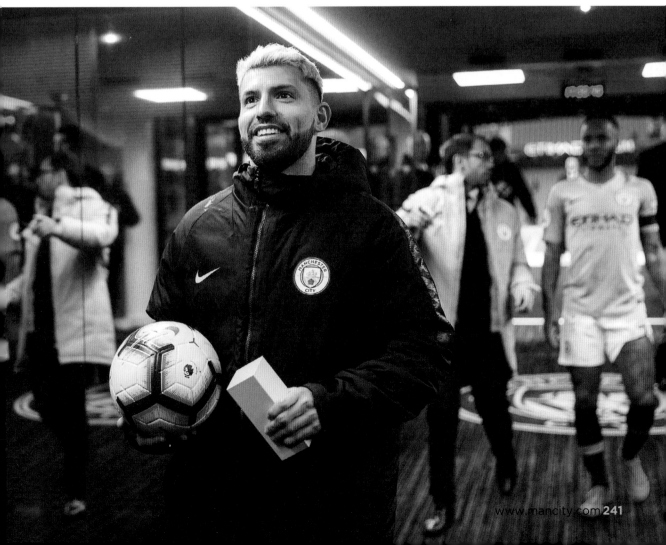

City won the Carabao Cup for the second year in succession after a penalty shootout victory over Chelsea at Wembley.

In a somewhat uninspired game, City failed to hit top gear, yet found a way to win the trophy for the fourth time in six years.

Sergio Aguero had one of the few decent chances of the afternoon, chesting the ball down from Bernardo Silva's cross before fizzing a shot over the bar.

City were the more adventurous side, but Chelsea sat deep and made life difficult with the men from Stamford Bridge seeking to avoid a repeat of the 6-0 defeat they had suffered at the Etihad just a fortnight earlier.

Chelsea finally threatened on 53 minutes when Eden Hazard

Chelsea 0-0 City
(City win 4-3 on penalties)
SHOOTOUT WIN SEES CITY LIFT CARABAO CUP AGAIN
24 February 2019

broke clear into the box, only to be tackled superbly by Nicolas Otamendi. It was a perfectly-timed challenge from the Argentine.

Indeed, the match is most likely to be remembered for a bizarre incident that saw Chelsea goalkeeper Kepa Arrizabalaga publicly defy manager Maurizio Sarri's attempt to substitute him shortly before the shootout.

In the ensuing shootout, Ederson saved Jorginho's spot-kick and David Luiz hit the post, before Raheem Sterling scored the decisive penalty to seal victory.

It was yet another example of the City forward's ability to make significant contributions. Sterling had been electric all season, and two months before this game had been subjected to racist abuse from a Chelsea supporter in City's 2-0 league defeat at Stamford Bridge.

Sterling's mental fortitude could not be questioned, and he was having a phenomenal season for City once again.

Our second successive Carabao Cup success was the sixth in our history, moving us clear of Aston Villa, Manchester United and Chelsea (five wins each) into second place on the list of all-time winners. Only Liverpool (eight) had won the trophy more times in the competition's history.

"I'm happy," manager Pep Guardiola declared afterwards. "It went to penalties, so compliments to Chelsea, it was an incredible performance. In penalties, everything can happen. We are happy to win back-to-back [League Cups] for the first time in our history.

"You realise the team Chelsea have, they have champions. After the result two weeks ago, we knew it would be more difficult.

The only bad thing is we will miss players in the next weeks. I don't know how far we can arrive with Laporte and Fernandinho injured, but it's better after winning the game.

"The important thing with penalties is personality, and they did it."

Bernardo Silva delivered a fine display, mixing artistry, outstanding technique and hard work to lethal effect. On a day when little quality shone through, the Portuguese playmaker stood out as the most inventive player on the pitch.

It was by no means a classic City performance – we came nowhere near the level we managed in the 6-0 win over the Londoners in the Premier League two weeks earlier.

But, as is the hallmark of all great teams, we found a way to win.

Manchester United 0-2 City

OLD TRAFFORD VICTORY LEAVES TITLE RACE IN CITY'S HANDS

24 April 2019

With four games left of the 2018-19 season, City knew four wins to finish would seal a second consecutive title ahead of a phenomenal Liverpool side.

The first of those four assignments saw us travel to Old Trafford, once a venue that instilled fear but one that in recent years had become a happy hunting ground for us.

City produced a fine display, winning 2-0, to return to the top of the table with three matches remaining as we made it a remarkable 11 straight Premier League victories. Extend that run to 14, and the title would be ours for a second year in succession, regardless of what Liverpool produced.

This was our seventh Premier League win at Old Trafford, a feat no other club had managed, with Pep Guardiola becoming the first manager to win three consecutive away matches at United's ground since the inception of the Premier League in 1992.

City should have been ahead in the first half, and it was a bold tactical move that was perhaps the catalyst for the win. With the score locked at 0-0, Fernandinho was withdrawn due

to injury after 51 minutes. Leroy Sané replaced him as Guardiola rejigged his forward line. The switch worked like a dream, with City far more menacing for the remainder of the game.

Our first goal came courtesy of Bernardo Silva, who received the ball on the right-hand side, advanced into the area, cut onto his left and struck past David De Gea at the goalkeeper's near post.

Sergio Aguero struck the post after a fine one-touch passing move from City, before Sané bagged our second, firing home after fine work from Raheem Sterling. Could De Gea have done better? City didn't care one bit.

In combining for the second goal, it meant Leroy Sané (10 goals, 10 assists) and Raheem Sterling (17 goals, 10 assists) had both reached double figures in goals and assists in the league this season. Only one other player, Chelsea's Eden Hazard, had managed that particular milestone.

The victory meant City had now scored 157 goals in all competitions this season – the most by an English top-flight side in a single season. And we weren't just winning; we were doing so in swashbuckling style.

Even United manager Ole Gunnar Solskjaer was impressed with City's quality and consistency.

"They are the best team in the country," he acknowledged. "They have set the standard in the last two seasons, and I don't know how many points they've taken.

"What Pep Guardiola has done with his players is remarkable and we are so close to it – in the vicinity – so we feel it every day."

There were, understandably, scenes of jubilation at the final whistle as the City players made their way over to the away end to thank the travelling supporters. The job was by no means done – Liverpool were providing formidable opposition that meant slip ups were not an option – but this was another significant hurdle cleared.

A visibly delighted Guardiola said City's improved second-half display had been key.

"We play with a lot of pressure," he said. "They were playing for Champions League qualification. After their 4-0 defeat by Everton, we knew their players would be committed.

"We lost some balls in the middle of the pitch in the first half and they had counter-attacks. We did well to win the game in the second half. Fortunately, we made an incredible second half."

Now there were just three games left: Burnley (away), Leicester (home) and Brighton (away). Nine points from those fixtures and we would become the first team in a decade to retain the Premier League title.

City 1-0 Leicester City

KOMPANY'S ICONIC STRIKE EDGES CITY CLOSER TO TITLE

6 May 2019

I f ever a moment summed up a player and their contribution to Manchester City, this was it.

There were cries of "don't shoot!" as Vincent Kompany, a central defender with a sum total of 19 City goals in 11 years, shaped up to pull the trigger from 30 yards.

The reticence was understandable. None of Kompany's goals had come from outside the area and this was a night of extreme importance. Leicester's visit to the Etihad was the penultimate match of our Premier League season. A win would take us into the final fixture, away at Brighton, knowing victory would seal back-to-back titles. Dropped points, however, would allow Liverpool to assume control, an opportunity they were unlikely to spurn.

There was no room for error. Games very rarely have more riding on them, and when Kompany lined up his shot with just 20 minutes remaining, the score was 0-0 – the longest City had gone without scoring in a match all season. The tension inside the Etihad was high.

But Kompany, in the latest example of his sheer bloody-mindedness, did shoot. And not just any old shot, but one that flew off his foot sweetly and arrowed into the top corner at bullet speed in what was one of the most exhilarating moments in City's history.

It was a sensational strike – a decisive contribution in a time of severe need.

"Where do you want your statue, Vincent Kompany!" was the famous cry from Sky Sports pundit Gary Neville.

"An incredible player," was manager Pep Guardiola's post-match verdict on his captain.

The euphoric celebrations told their own story. Kompany ran screaming to the corner flag and slid towards the jubilant City fans. His teammates sprinted after him to join in. Pandemonium ripped through the stands.

It had been a night of almost unbearable tension, one defined by the nervousness that pervaded the ground. Leicester had almost gone ahead late on when former City striker Kelechi Iheanacho fired wide when clean through and almost certain to score. Indeed, Brendan Rodgers' side were exceptional, a team full of pace, movement and clever passing.

But Kompany's goal, fittingly City's 100th in all competitions at the Etihad that season – which extended our record for most home goals by an English top-flight team in a single campaign – settled the game and saw us go into the final day one point ahead of Liverpool.

"One game left, and it will be so tough like today," Guardiola said afterwards. "We are away and we saw Brighton had a good game at Arsenal. But it is in our hands, don't forget we could have been 10 points behind if we lost to Liverpool here [in January]."

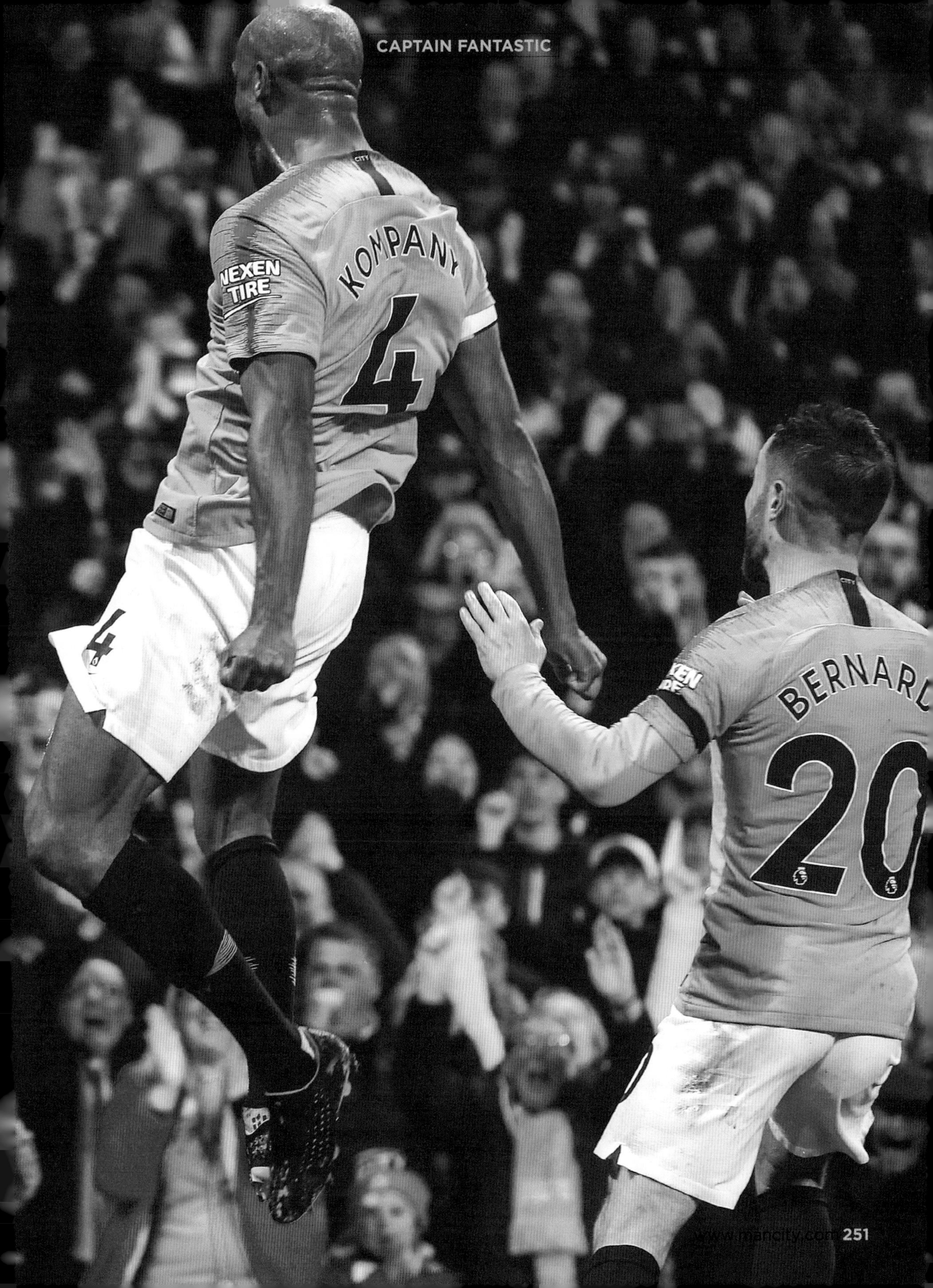
NEXEN TIRE
KOMPANY
4
BERNARD
20

"We were seven points behind, but now we are in the last game and it is in our hands. We are going to prepare well. We'll see if Brighton defend deep or will be more offensive. It will be tough, but hopefully we will have the performance to be champions."

After the game, the traditional final-day lap of honour took place. Kompany looked emotionally drained as he waved to the adoring City supporters. Little did we know, he was saying goodbye to the home fans for good. The Belgian would subsequently announce he was leaving City, after 11 years and 12 trophies, at the end of the season.

The win over Leicester was our 13th in a row in the league and it had taken us to the brink of becoming the first side in 10 years to retain the Premier League title. It also meant we had beaten every team in the league for the second consecutive season; the only other English top-flight team to achieve the feat were Preston between 1888-89 and 1889-90.

Here's to you, Vincent Kompany.

Brighton 1-4 City

BACK-TO-BACK TITLES SECURED IN STYLE

12 May 2019

Manchester City became the first side in 10 years to retain the Premier League title after a 4-1 win away at Brighton on the final day of the 2018-19 season.

City knew victory would see us edge out Liverpool, regardless of their result against Wolves at Anfield.

Despite going behind to a Glenn Murray strike after 27 minutes, City never really looked in danger.

Sergio Aguero restored parity 83 seconds later with his 32nd goal of the season in all competitions and from there Pep Guardiola's side were both ruthless and dazzling.

Aymeric Laporte's header deservedly put City ahead before half-time, with Riyad Mahrez extending the lead with a fine strike just past the hour mark.

And Ilkay Gundogan's brilliant free-kick sealed the win, with City utterly dominant, managing 76% possession and 20 shots to Brighton's six.

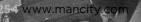

This was the third time City had won the title in the final day of the season and the celebrations in the away end at full-time were euphoric.

After storming to the title the previous season – finishing the campaign with a 19-point winning margin – this success had been far more complicated. Liverpool's 97 points – the highest tally ever posted by a second-placed Premier League team – had pushed City all the way, with every game during the final months of the season fraught and tense.

Liverpool lost just once all term, but our amazing 14-game winning run to finish the campaign, a new record

eclipsing Arsenal's record of 13 straight victories, saw us pip one of the Premier League's finest ever sides to the post.

To have managed 198 points across two seasons in the most competitive league in world football was remarkable, something Guardiola said he was incredibly proud to have achieved.

"We have to say congratulations to Liverpool and thank you so much, they pushed us to increase our standards," the City boss said afterwards.

"It's incredible, 98 points, to go back-to-back. We made the standard higher last season and Liverpool helped

us. To win this title we had to win 14 (league games) in a row. We couldn't lose one point."

Raheem Sterling, who scored 17 goals and assisted 12 in the Premier League throughout the 2018-19 season, said this title win was another example of why he came to City and singled out Mahrez, who was the man of the match at the Amex, for special praise.

"I'm just delighted, this is exactly what I came to the club for, to win trophies and be in these moments," Sterling declared.

"The manager here... his mentality is the best. It's always about winning. It's

the way he sets us up. I'm happy to be here learning and winning.

"As a manager, he's got multiple players in each position challenging each other. No one is comfortable here but everyone is ready to take their chance – like Riyad today. He's not played much recently but I knew he was going to score today."

City now had the chance to complete the first-ever domestic treble in English football, with the FA Cup final against Watford at Wembley just six days away. History beckoned, and on the evidence of what we saw at Brighton, nothing could stop us from completing the set.

2018-19 PREMIER LEAGUE CHAMPIONS: THE STATS

FIRST IN A DECADE

City are the first side since Manchester United a decade ago to retain the Premier League title.

98	City's remarkable 98 points means we dropped just 16 all season.
198	That means over the course of the 2017-18 and 2018-19 seasons, City amassed 198 Premier League points, which is 26 more than Liverpool, in second, have managed in the same period. To drop just 30 points in two years in the world's most competitive league highlights our remarkable consistency.

TAKING ON ALL-COMERS

City are the first side since Preston to claim at least one league victory against every side they have faced in two consecutive seasons.

32	City also equalled the Premier League record, set by us during the Centurions campaign, for the most wins in a single campaign: 32. What's more, the lead at the top of the table changed hands a record-breaking 32 times in what turned out to be the most keenly fought battle for the Premier League in recent memory.
14	City are the first team to end a top-flight campaign with 14 consecutive victories, breaking Arsenal's record of 13 set in 2001-02. Only that level of consistency was going to see us fend off Liverpool's challenge, and it's a stat that underlines the mental fortitude in our squad. There was no margin for error, but we managed to get over the line.
97	Liverpool's tally of 97 would have been enough to win the Premier League every year except the last two. It's the highest runners-up tally in the history of the competition. This is the first time two sides has amassed 90+ points in a single season.
95	City scored 95 goals in the league during 2018-19, six more than nearest challengers Liverpool.

City 6-0 Watford

CITY SEAL DOMESTIC CLEAN-SWEEP WITH FA CUP SUCCESS

18 May 2019

City rounded off the greatest campaign in the club's history by beating Watford 6-0 in the FA Cup final.

No side had ever won the Premier League, FA Cup, League Cup and Community Shield in a single season, but City became the first to achieve the historic clean sweep after an utterly dominant display at Wembley.

The result also saw us equal the record for the biggest win in an FA Cup final - the only other six-goal margin coming way back in 1903 when Bury defeated Derby 6-0 at the Crystal Palace Stadium.

"It was an incredible final for us, and we have finished an incredible year," manager Pep Guardiola said after winning his sixth trophy since taking over as City boss in 2016.

"To all the people at the club, a big congratulations, especially the players because they are the reason why we have won these titles."

50 years after our famous FA Cup triumph under Joe Mercer, which saw us defeat Leicester 1-0 thanks to Neil Young's iconic strike, Guardiola's class of 2019 showed their own quality to etch their names in the history books.

Ederson made a fine save from Gerard Deulofeu in the opening moments, with City somewhat on the back foot.

But David Silva, lashing home his tenth goal of the season with a fine first-time finish past Heurelho Gomes, gave us the lead after 26 minutes – a strike that saw him become just the second City player in history to score in both an FA Cup and League Cup final.

The dynamic of the game changed

drastically thereafter, with City assuming complete control.

Gabriel Jesus, making his 100th appearance for the club, doubled our lead five minutes before half-time, latching on to a fine ball to the back post from the irrepressible Bernardo Silva.

Kevin De Bruyne, who came on as a substitute after 55 minutes and still managed to win the man-of-the-match award, made it 3-0 moments after arriving on the pitch. He collected a square ball from Jesus, rounded Gomes and slotted home. A moment of typical class from the Belgian.

Jesus' second, a cool finish past Gomes, put City in total command, before Raheem Sterling's late double completed the rout and saw us lift the FA Cup for the sixth time in the club's history.

It meant City had scored 26 goals en route to lifting the trophy, the most by any team in a single FA Cup campaign since 1946.

And our excellence over the course of a memorable campaign was further highlighted by the fact we became the first English top-flight side to register 50 wins in all competitions in a single season.

Skipper Vincent Kompany, who the following day

announced he would leave City after 11 trophy-laden years at the club, said he felt City were now the best team in world football.

"It wasn't as easy as the score makes it look. But what a season, what a tremendous club," he said.

"It started with the manager; he sets the standard at the start of the season. It's the best team in the world for me. To set such a high standard for so long - not just for one year but two years running now."

The result marked the end of a momentous season for City, who scored 169 goals in all competitions, a new record for a top-flight English side.

This was the first time a team had won a Premier League and FA Cup double since Chelsea did it under Carlo Ancelotti in 2009-10 – but by adding the League Cup to our collection too, we had broken new ground.

Centurions in 2017-18 and Fourmidables in 2018-19, City had changed the landscape of English football with a consistency and brilliance never before seen on these shores.

City 8-0 Watford

NEW CLUB RECORD ON CITY'S 125TH ANNIVERSARY

21 September 2019

City scored five goals in the first 18 minutes of the game as we overwhelmed Watford 8-0 on the day the club celebrated its 125th anniversary.

It was City's biggest ever top-flight win, with the 18-minute blitz the fastest any side has gone 5-0 ahead in a Premier League match.

City became only the seventh team to win a top-flight game by an eight-goal margin in the modern era thanks to a ruthless display.

"After 30 seconds we realised it would be tough, after 10 minutes really difficult and after 15 minutes it was impossible," forlorn Watford boss Quique Sanchez Flores reflected afterwards.

David Silva opened the scoring on 52 seconds with the fastest goal in the Premier League of the season, before Sergio Aguero's penalty made it 2-0 after seven minutes.

It was Aguero's 100th Premier League goal at the Etihad, making him one of only three players in the competition's history to net 100+ goals at a single venue, alongside Thierry Henry at Highbury (114) and Wayne Rooney at Old Trafford (101).

Five minutes later, Riyad Mahrez struck via a deflection, before Bernardo Silva nodded home his first of the afternoon and Nicolas Otamendi slid in at the back post to tap in our fifth.

"It is not normal to score five goals with five shots like we did," manager Pep Guardiola admitted afterwards. "But the quality of the players up front made a difference."

Bernardo completed his hat-trick with two second-half goals, before man of the match Kevin De Bruyne finished the rout with a powerful drive into the top corner from just inside the area.

This was our twelfth successive win against Watford, with City having scored 33 goals in seven matches between the sides.

After losing to Norwich the previous week, City had bounced back superbly, beating Shakhtar Donetsk 3-0 away from home in the Champions League before this scintillating display against Watford.

"People still don't understand - journalists, pundits, former players – that losing games is part of life," stressed Guardiola.

"Opponents always deserve respect. The same feeling I have now, I had after Norwich, so it was not a bad performance last week.

"We can lose the games, but the important thing is the approach and how we react."

It was a fitting performance on a day of celebration for City. September marked the historic milestone of our first league game and league win in 1894, and the Watford fixture was chosen to mark the auspicious occasion, 125 years on.

Community spirit has been a key facet of a Club founded by the parishioners of St Mark's Church – inspired by the work of the Connell family – who believed that forming a football club could improve the lives of those within their community. Their commendable legacy and spirit live on with us today.

Fittingly, in May 1894, at the Football League AGM held in Manchester, Manchester City secretary Joshua Parlby make a passionate speech about Manchester's need for a Football League club on the same day Queen Victoria officially opened the Ship Canal. Parlby's eloquence has been remembered for decades as the reason City were accepted.

The following September, City faced Bury on the first of the month in our first league game, before hosting Burton Wanderers at Hyde Road in our maiden home clash.

Our first victory arrived with a 4-1 triumph over Burslem Port Vale on 8 September, and Club hero Billy Meredith signed in October. The legendary Welsh wizard went on to score his opening goals for City in the inaugural Football League Manchester derby the following November.

In commemoration of those first fixtures 125 years ago, special events took place at the Etihad before, during and after the match against the Hornets to celebrate.

The players certainly turned on the style for those in attendance.

Manchester United 1-3 City

SUPER CITY DELIVER DERBY MASTERCLASS IN SEMI-FINAL FIRST LEG

7 January 2020

City took a giant step towards a third straight Carabao Cup final after a superb first leg semi-final win over Manchester United at Old Trafford.

Pep Guardiola's impressive side outclassed our rivals, particularly in the first half where the gulf between the two sides had rarely felt wider. City, led by the dynamism and running power of Bernardo Silva, were imperious.

Guardiola's team selection raised some eyebrows. City played without a conventional striker, instead employing Bernardo and Kevin De Bruyne as the furthest players forward in a system that was striker-less but potent.

The ploy worked perfectly, with the beguiling movement of our midfield players proving too much for United to handle.

There was a fluidity to City's play that made us irresistible; United spent much of the first half chasing shadows.

City were 3-0 up at half-time after a magnificent first 45 minutes. Bernardo set us on our way with a brilliant left-footed strike that arrowed past David De Gea into the top corner.

Riyad Mahrez then latched on to a magnificent through ball from Bernardo, rounded De Gea before doubling our advantage.

And a breathless counter-attack five minutes later ended with City 3-0 up. Swift one-touch passing took City from the edge of their own area to inside United's in a flash. De Bruyne turned Phil Jones inside out and left him on the ground, before seeing his effort saved by De Gea, hit Andreas Pereira and go in.

There were wild scenes of celebration in the away end, with a reduced number of 3,000 City fans, who were superb all evening, revelling in their team's mastery.

The only surprise was City didn't inflict further damage.

United were booed off at half-time for their efforts but came out more determined after the break and Marcus Rashford's reply gave them some hope ahead of the second leg.

It was City's seventh win in 10 away matches against United in all competitions, as many as we had managed in our previous 42 visits to Old Trafford.

Given City's commanding lead going into the home leg, many felt the tie was as good as over. Especially as given the past 15 teams to win away from home in the first leg of a League Cup semi-final had all progressed to the final.

However, Guardiola stressed afterwards that nothing was decided yet.

"The last game against United [a 2-1 loss in December] we could not control when we lost the ball, and tonight we did it better," the City manager said afterwards. "We lost the ball in a position which is so dangerous [for the United goal]. We cannot forget which team we play. Tonight we can be more than satisfied to come here to Old Trafford and win.

"It is not over. We have one more game and we'll see what happens. Of course Manchester United can come back. Last year here they lost to Paris St-Germain [in the Champions League] and qualified. They have the shirt which means history and pride."

It was a magnificent performance of free-flowing, creative football. Bernardo was the star, but Fernandinho at centre-half, De Bruyne playing as a false nine and Mahrez's pace and skill were all in premium form, too.

A night to remember.

Aston Villa 1-2 City

FODEN INSPIRES CITY TO CARABAO CUP HAT-TRICK

1 March 2020

City retained the Carabao Cup with a 2-1 win over Aston Villa at Wembley.

It was our third consecutive success in the competition – and fifth in seven years – with our remarkable grip on the trophy remaining tight.

City broke the deadlock after 20 minutes. Rodri flighted a teasing ball towards Phil Foden, who guided a beautifully cushioned header to Sergio Aguero, and he fired the ball into the ground and past Orjan Nyland.

Foden almost made it 2-0 when he deftly killed a cross-field pass from Oleksandr Zinchenko, skipped inside Matt Targett and shot just wide.

But City didn't have to wait long for a second. Our growing dominance was rewarded again just shy of the half-hour mark when Rodri produced a thumping header from Ilkay Gundogan's corner to give Nyland no chance.

Villa's Mbwana Samatta powered home with a spectacular diving header on 41 minutes to narrow the deficit and give City some thinking to do at half-time.

Our domination continued in the second half, but we could not find a crucial third goal to kill the game off. Foden saw a half-volley narrowly miss the target and Rodri's header forced a superb save from Nyland.

Disaster was averted when Claudio Bravo produced a late moment of magic, the City 'keeper pushing Bjorn Engels' goalbound header onto the post in a nerve-shredding finale.

However, City held on to seal a deserved Carabao Cup hat-trick.

Foden was the stand-out player for City, delivering a virtuoso display of vision, skill and maturity. He set up the opener with a beautiful, cushioned header and was central to everything we did thereafter.

The victory marked our eighth successive victory at Wembley across all competitions – a remarkable run that stretched back to our Carabao Cup final win in 2018.

"Three times in a row is a big success. It's the consistency, incredible," manager Pep Guardiola remarked after the game. "It was awesome. We struggled in the first minutes and the last ones. They had two clear chances in the first minutes but we played really well, especially in the second half.

"The game was good. Phil [Foden] was clinical. Big success, our second title of the season with the Community Shield, it's so nice. We've won a lot. I tried when we arrived, every game we play we try to win it, every competition we try to win it, and three times in a row, being here and winning is great."

City's victory was an especially memorable occasion for Sergio Aguero, Fernandinho and David Silva.

It marked a fifth Carabao Cup success for the illustrious City trio – a truly remarkable record of achievement and the perfect testament to their supreme talent and professionalism.

All three had now played a key role in our League Cup triumphs in 2014, 2016, 2018, 2019 and 2020.

KEY POST-MATCH STATS

- City had now won six consecutive English trophies.

- This was our seventh League Cup success (1970, 1976, 2014, 2016, 2018, 2019, 2020).

- Guardiola had now won 21 of the 25 finals he had overseen as a top-flight manager – including six with City (one FA Cup, three League Cups and two Community Shields).

- At this point City had progressed or won the final of each of our previous 19 domestic English cup ties (FA/League Cup).

- City's fifth League Cup in seven seasons.

- Aguero had scored 10 goals in his past six starts against Aston Villa.

RUBEN DIAS

The only player profiled in this book who has spent just one season at the club is Ruben Dias. However, such was his impact over the course of the 2020-21 campaign, his inclusion felt more than justified.

He joined from Benfica; a club renowned for exporting high-quality players. With a Vincent Kompany-shaped vacuum at the heart of our defence, City had needed a world-class centre-half for more than a year. Dias had been monitored closely for some time by the club's scouting network but surely no one could have predicted the impact he would have.

> "The most important thing to say is I love to win and that is the thing you most need to know about me"

"The most important thing to say is I love to win and that is the thing you most need to know about me," Dias said in his first interview as a City player. As statements of intent go, Dias could not have been clearer, but those words could have sounded awfully hollow had he not delivered one of the most consistent debut seasons in English football's recent history.

He is the full package, a player with strength, maturity, exceptional reading of the game and a turn of speed when needed. He is also comfortable on the ball, making him an ideal fit for Pep Guardiola's system. And it isn't just the quality of Dias' game that has made him so vital to City in such a short space of time; his leadership also brought some much-needed

regeneration to our defensive line.

He's also the ultimate pro and one of the most naturally fit and athletic players in City's squad. Always one of the first on the training field and regularly in the gym afterwards, he rarely misses a game and is teetotal. Asked once whether he had yet tried a cup of tea, a ritual for those living in the north of England, he explained he only drinks two things: water and fruit juice. The way he fuels his body is of the utmost importance.

The 24-year-old's impact was instant – a fine debut away at Leeds United setting the tone. City came into the game fresh from conceding five at home to Leicester, with serious question marks being asked about our backline but immediately looked tougher and more assured with Dias in the ranks.

By the end of his first season at City, he had been central to us winning the Premier League title and League Cup, as well as reaching our first ever Champions League final. He played 50 times in all competitions, with City winning 75% of them and keeping a clean sheet in 45% (conceding just 29 in total). His influence was seismic.

He was named the FWA Footballer of the Year, the Premier League Player of the Year and the Etihad Player of the Year – a trio of personal accolades that underlined his enormous effect and importance.

We're looking at a potential world star, someone who could perhaps take the baton from Europe's best centre-back of the last generation, Sergio Ramos, and lay down his own legacy. His first season at City suggests he has what it takes to do just that.

Chelsea 1-3 City

CITY FIND GROOVE WITH SUPERB PERFORMANCE AT STAMFORD BRIDGE

3 January 2021

The context could not have been more difficult.

City travelled to Chelsea for our first fixture of 2021 with a depleted squad. Our previous game, away at Everton, had been postponed after a round of Covid-19 testing returned a number of positive cases, in addition to the four already reported on Christmas Day.

With the security of the bubble compromised, there posed a risk that the virus could spread further amongst the squad, the staff and potentially beyond.

Based on strong medical advice, the Premier League, in consultation with both clubs, postponed the fixture.

The City Football Academy reopened two days later but we were without Kyle Walker, Gabriel Jesus, Ederson, Ferran Torres, Eric Garcia and Tommy Doyle for the game against Chelsea.

Going into the game at Stamford Bridge, City sat eighth in the Premier League table, despite 10 wins in succession, after a difficult start to the season saw us drop as low as 12th at one stage.

But against a backdrop of absence, illness and chaotic preparations, City produced a mesmeric performance to beat Chelsea 3-1 and move up to fifth in the table.

In truth, the game was effectively over as a contest after three goals in 16 ruthless first-half minutes that blew Chelsea away.

Strikes from Ilkay Gundogan, Phil Foden and Kevin De Bruyne meant there was no way back for the hosts who were outplayed for most of the match before pulling a goal back with almost the last kick.

A clearly delighted City boss Pep Guardiola was full of praise for his players who had shown resilience and brilliance in equal measure.

"We played really well," he said. "It's unfortunate about the last goal but the result at Stamford Bridge is fantastic. Today we were back like we were two or three seasons ago. An important win at Chelsea away.

"The Premier League is weird for everything [this season]. We just have to be focused during the games but otherwise relax. Hopefully in the Premier League in the last six, seven games we can be there fighting."

It was a crucial afternoon for the club. The victory at Chelsea appeared to kick-start City's belief and we looked a much more accomplished side from then on as we closed in on our third title in four years.

"It was the turning point, definitely," Guardiola reflected in April 2021, with his side 11 points clear at the top of the Premier League table.

"At Stamford Bridge, with just 14 players available, injuries and Covid, that was the moment we believed we could do it. That was one of the three moments earlier in the season that helped us stay there – but the Chelsea win helped us think we can do it."

City's character and resilience had shone through, providing a result that had a significant effect on our season. Three days later, we would travel to Manchester United for a one-off Carabao Cup semi-final.

Manchester United 0-2 City

OLD TRAFFORD VICTORY DEDICATED TO COLIN BELL

6 January 2021

City produced a fine performance to see off Manchester United at Old Trafford in the last four of the Carabao Cup and reach the final of the competition for the fourth season in a row.

John Stones steered in Phil Foden's free-kick to give Pep Guardiola's side the lead early in the second half and Fernandinho fired in a 20-yard volley to seal a deserved victory and our place in the final, where we would meet Tottenham Hotspur.

It was a dominant display from City and the victory – in what was a one-off semi-final – was dedicated to club legend Colin Bell, who had sadly passed away the day before the game.

Bell, an iconic figure in City's history, died after a short, non-Covid related illness, aged 74.

He is widely regarded to be the finest City player of his generation, making 501 appearances and scoring 153 goals during a wonderful 13-year stay.

Few players have left such an indelible mark on City.

Known as Colin The King, in 2004 City fans voted to name a stand inside the Etihad Stadium after him and his name is still sung regularly at matches.

"It was a sad day for all of the Manchester City family," manager Pep Guardiola said after the game. "We are in the present now, but the past was created by great players. Colin has a stand in the Etihad Stadium and was called The King because he was special.

"This game is dedicated to Colin Bell. A great night for us and one dedicated to Colin and his family."

Stones proved the star man at Old Trafford, with his goal that set City on the way to victory topping off a fine defensive performance from a player very much in form.

He handled United's attackers with aplomb and displayed his customary calm on the ball, continually stepping into midfield to launch City attacks. In this kind of form, there are few Premier League defenders who offer more.

"John Stones came back; he made another outstanding performance," added Guardiola. "But the most important thing he has been able to do – something he has struggled with the past few years – is to play four, five, six games in a row. This is so important – for him especially, and for us.

"All the team was incredible."

The result saw City become only the second side to reach four consecutive League Cup finals, after Liverpool who achieved the feat between 1981 and 1984.

A win over Spurs in the final would see us draw level with Liverpool on eight League Cup wins. History beckoned.

Liverpool 1-4 City

LONG-AWAITED ANFIELD WIN STRENGTHENS TITLE CHANCES

7 February 2021

Eighteen years is a very long time in football.

Not since Nicolas Anelka's double for Kevin Keegan's Manchester City back in May 2003 had we tasted success at Anfield.

In the intervening period, we hadn't just failed to win – we'd suffered badly. Even Pep Guardiola hadn't been able to change our fortunes at Liverpool's home in his first four seasons, with painful defeats in both the Premier League and Champions League still smarting in particular.

For that record to change, a big performance was needed and that's exactly what we got in February 2021 as a virtuoso display from Phil Foden propelled City to a memorable 4-1 win and strengthened our lead at the top of the Premier League table.

Foden was magical, delivering his finest performance to date for City, one defined by intelligence and ignited by his outrageous skill and ability. There aren't many young players in world football who can compete with him in terms of talent.

His touch and feel have been obvious since he was a child in our Academy, but at Anfield he showed maturity and muscle, too.

City controlled things from the off, but Ilkay Gundogan skied his first-half spot-kick after Fabinho had fouled Raheem Sterling inside the box. After Riyad Mahrez's missed penalty the year before, which had denied us a win we thoroughly deserved, this felt like an ominous omen.

But Gundogan had emerged as one of City's most important players in recent months and he made amends in the second half, firing home after Liverpool goalkeeper Alisson had palmed away Foden's initial close-range effort.

A penalty from Mohamed Salah saw Liverpool equalise just past the hour after Ruben Dias had tugged the forward's arm.

Moments later, Foden flighted a brilliant ball into the box that John Stones tapped home from close range – but it was ruled out after the tightest of offside calls.

At that point, it felt like another tale of woe was emerging, with City dominating but the score level.

But Foden illustrated his genius soon after. Two poor clearances from Alisson put Liverpool under pressure, and Foden went on a mesmerising run into the box before rolling the ball across for Gundogan to tap home his second.

Another loose ball from Alisson saw City make it 3-1. Bernardo Silva intercepted after the Liverpool goalkeeper tried to pass out from his own six-yard box, and the Portuguese playmaker then scooped the ball over Alisson's head for Raheem Sterling to head home.

Our fourth was the pick of the bunch. A wonderful passing sequence ended with Gabriel Jesus playing the ball wide to Foden, who skipped inside Andrew Robertson before unleashing a rasping drive into the roof of the net.

It was a goal of extreme quality, but one befitting Foden's mercurial display.

"I have a lot of emotions, many things happening in the game," Guardiola reflected. "Gundogan missed a penalty – it's like a routine against them – but we started really, really well, doing what we want to do.

"In the second half, the way we reacted to the goal, the way we played with quality, made the difference.

"For many years we were not able to win here. Hopefully next time we can do it with people. Anfield is so intimidating.

The result sent City five points clear at the top with a game in hand over second-placed Manchester United – and extended our lead over reigning champions Liverpool to 10 points having played a game less.

It may have been a long time coming, but City, inspired by Foden, had finally ended our Anfield hoodoo.

City 4-1 Wolves

CITY EXTEND ENGLISH FOOTBALL WIN RECORD

2 March 2021

" **In winter time in England it's hell and in that time we did something incredible. It's more than remarkable."**
That was Pep Guardiola's striking assessment after City's 4-1 win over Wolves at the Etihad Stadium, a triumph that saw us extend the English top-flight record for consecutive victories in all competitions.

City had now won 21 matches in succession, a period which had seen us move 15 points clear at the top of the Premier League table, reach the final of the League Cup, the quarter-finals of the FA Cup and taken control of our last-16 Champions League tie against Borussia Moenchengladbach.

It was a remarkable sequence of results in which we had scored 55 goals and conceded just eight, becoming only the third team from the big-five European leagues to record more than 20 consecutive victories, after Bayern Munich (23 in 2020) and Real Madrid (22 in 2014).

A Leander Dendoncker own goal put City 1-0 up in the first half, but Conor Coady equalised against the run of play on the hour mark.

City were not to be denied, however. Gabriel Jesus smashed home from close range after Kyle Walker's cross was deflected into his path to restore our lead, before man of the match Riyad Mahrez reacted quickest inside the area to drive a loose ball past Rui Patricio.

Jesus grabbed his second and City's fourth in the final seconds, tapping in after Ilkay Gundogan's 20-yard effort was parried back into his path.

"We were little bit anxious after 1-1 but we reacted really well after we scored the goals. It was well deserved – we played really good. The games are tight and in the last minutes we win the game comfortably," Guardiola added.

"After 1-1, they were dangerous, but we continued to take the ball and we didn't give up and that's a good lesson for us in the little details. When you see the performance, we were really good."

Despite a gruelling fixture list caused by our continued involvement in four competitions and the COVID-19 pandemic, City looked fresh. Guardiola's rotation policy, which had seen City make more changes to the starting line-up than any other Premier League side (79), was paying dividends.

Mahrez was the man of the match, registering a goal and assist, as well as tormenting the Wolves backline with his pace and quick feet. He had now been directly involved in 30 goals in 38 starts in all competitions for City at the Etihad (15 goals, 15 assists).

Against the backdrop of a global health pandemic and the restrictions it had caused, City's consistency had surprised everyone. Defeat in our next match to Manchester United ended hopes of setting a new European record for consecutive wins, but we stood seven clear of our nearest challengers in English football, the Arsenal team of 1987 who managed 14 straight wins across all competitions.

LONGEST WINNING RUNS FOR ENGLISH TOP-FLIGHT SIDES
(all competitions)

DATES	TEAM	LONGEST WINNING RUNS
9/12/20 – 2/3/2021	MAN CITY	21
12/09/1987 to 17/11/1987	Arsenal	14
24/10/1891 to 30/01/1892	Preston North End	14
23/03/2002 to 18/08/2002	Arsenal	13
23/04/1960 to 01/10/1960	Spurs	13
16/03/2000 to 06/05/2000	Arsenal	12
25/08/2007 to 23/10/2007	Arsenal	12
24/03/1894 to 13/10/1894	Everton	12
25/08/2018 to 25/10/2018	Arsenal	11
20/03/1897 to 18/09/1897	Aston Villa	11
10/01/1914 to 14/03/1914	Aston Villa	11
18/02/1989 to 11/04/1989	Liverpool	11
15/03/2006 to 07/05/2006	Liverpool	11
19/04/2015 to 12/09/2015	MAN CITY	11
26/08/2017 to 21/10/2017	MAN CITY	11
10/10/1964 to 02/12/1964	Man United	11
11/01/2009 to 21/02/2009	Man United	11

City 1-0 Tottenham

LAPORTE'S LATE HEADER SECURES RECORD-EQUALLING EIGHTH LEAGUE CUP

25 April 2021

City won the League Cup for a record-equalling eighth time after beating Tottenham Hotspur 1-0 to lift the trophy for the fourth consecutive year.

Aymeric Laporte was City's hero, rising above Spurs substitute Moussa Sissoko to head home from Kevin De Bruyne's free-kick in the 82nd minute, giving Pep Guardiola's side a thoroughly deserved victory. It was De Bruyne 17th assist of the season, more than any other Premier League player had registered in all competitions.

City are only the second team to win the competition four times in a row, with this victory moving us level with Liverpool as the most successful side in the competition's history.

There were 8,000 supporters inside Wembley Stadium – the most at any game in England since the start of the COVID-19 pandemic – and Guardiola's men delivered a fine display for the City fans who had travelled to London.

City were the dominant side from the off and created the majority of the chances, with Spurs, under the guidance of caretaker manager Ryan Mason after the sacking of former boss Jose Mourinho earlier in the week, struggling to cope.

"This team in the last decade was the team in England – since Roberto Mancini won the Premier League, this team wins a lot of times," Guardiola said afterwards.

"It's nice, four Carabao Cups in a row, it means consistency in the team to be there. We beat Arsenal and Manchester United on the way so we can say we deserved to win this competition.

And a special day was given added significance by the fact Sergio Aguero and Fernandinho are now the most decorated players in the competition's history, with their six successes moving them one clear of Ian Rush and David Silva (both five).

"[It was] more than well deserved," Guardiola added. "We played with an incredible level and quality. I am so delighted for the guys and have a thought for those who couldn't play.

"Fernandinho and Sergio [Aguero], they are the players with the most cups and fourth time in a row is nice because we beat Arsenal and United away and Spurs to win it. It was more than deserved. It was a good night to share with our people, we are there."

Riyad Mahrez was City's star performer – and he was rightly awarded the official man of the match award after a performance of real quality that saw him frighten the Tottenham backline throughout with his pace and dribbling ability.

The result came eight days after City's defeat to Chelsea in the FA Cup semi-final ended our hopes of an unprecedented quadruple – and just three days before our Champions League semi-final first leg game away at Paris St-Germain.

"We are so happy to win this title again," Laporte said afterwards, having scored his most famous goal in a City shirt to date.

"This is very special for us because we lost in the FA Cup, it's good for us to get confidence. We have done so, so good in the last few months and we have to keep this rhythm to win more titles."

"We went out to play at an incredible level, with incredible quality," added Guardiola.

"We cannot deny one eye is always on the Champions League, but we take every game seriously, otherwise it is impossible to win four Carabao Cups in a row."

Guardiola is the first manager in history to win four League Cups in a row (2018-2021). Liverpool's four-successive wins came under two different managers, Bob Paisley (1981-83) and Joe Fagan (1984).

This was also Guardiola's 30th major trophy since becoming a manager.

The win over Tottenham also further reinforced City's remarkable consistency in the competition, extending our unbeaten League Cup run to 1,643 days. Not since a young City side lost to Manchester United at Old Trafford in October 2016 have we suffered a defeat.

In total, we'd won 22 out of 23 games in the competition since September 2017 (four of those coming in penalty shootouts after those matches finished in a draw), the only setback being a 1-0 loss to United in last season's Carabao Cup semi-final second leg.

Along the way, we've scored 53 goals, conceding just 13.

The League Cup has also provided the platform for a succession of exciting young players to receive their inaugural taste of first team football.

In total, 45 players have figured for the Club in that long unbeaten run – with the competition offering debuts to the likes of Oleksandr Zinchenko, Eric Garcia, Taylor Harwood-Bellis and Tommy Doyle.

CITY'S REMARKABLE UNBEATEN LEAGUE CUP RUN			
2017-18			
Third Round			
WEST BROMWICH	1	2	MANCHESTER CITY
Fourth Round			
MANCHESTER CITY	0	0	WOLVES
(City won 4-1 on pens)			
Quarter-final			
LEICESTER CITY	1	1	MANCHESTER CITY
(City won 4-3 on pens)			
Semi-final first leg			
MANCHESTER CITY	2	1	BRISTOL CITY
Semi-final second leg			
BRISTOL CITY	2	3	MANCHESTER CITY
(City won 5-3 on aggregate)			
Final			
ARSENAL	0	3	MANCHESTER CITY
2018-19			
Third Round			
OXFORD UNITED	0	3	MANCHESTER CITY
Fourth Round			
MANCHESTER CITY	2	0	FULHAM
Quarter-final			
LEICESTER CITY	1	1	MANCHESTER CITY
(City won 3-1 on pens)			
Semi-final first leg			
MANCHESTER CITY	9	0	BURTON ALBION
Semi-final second leg			
BURTON ALBION	0	1	MANCHESTER CITY
(City won 10-0 on aggregate)			
Final			
CHELSEA	0	0	MANCHESTER CITY
(City won 4-3 on pens)			
2019-20			
Third Round			
PRESTON NORTH END	0	3	MANCHESTER CITY
Fourth Round			
MANCHESTER CITY	3	1	SOUTHAMPTON
Quarter-final			
OXFORD UNITED	1	3	MANCHESTER CITY
Semi-final first leg			
MANCHESTER UNITED	1	3	MANCHESTER CITY
Semi-final second leg			
MANCHESTER CITY	0	1	MANCHESTER UNITED
(City won 3-2 on aggregate)			
Final			
MANCHESTER CITY	2	1	ASTON VILLA
2020-21			
Third Round			
MANCHESTER CITY	2	1	BOURNEMOUTH
Fourth Round			
BURNLEY	0	3	MANCHESTER CITY
Quarter-final			
ARSENAL	1	4	MANCHESTER CITY
Semi-final			
MANCHESTER UNITED	0	2	MANCHESTER CITY
Final			
MANCHESTER CITY	1	0	TOTTENHAM

City 2-0 Paris Saint-Germain

MAHREZ DOUBLE SECURES VICTORY ON MOMENTOUS EUROPEAN NIGHT

4 May 2021

City produced a dazzling display to move through to the Champions League final for the first time as Riyad Mahrez scored twice to seal a 2-0 semi-final second leg victory over Paris Saint-Germain, completing a 4-1 aggregate win.

Picking up where we left off in the second half of the first leg in Paris, City were exceptional; too quick, sharp and inventive for PSG to live with on a night that saw unseasonal snowfall in Manchester.

Our first goal was started by Ederson, who produced a 60-yard pass of pinpoint accuracy to set Oleksandr Zinchenko free down the left. The Ukrainian's square ball found Kevin De Bruyne at the edge of the area, his shot was blocked by Alessandro Florenzi, but Mahrez fired home expertly from a tight angle on the rebound.

City's second was arguably even more impressive, an ultra-swift counter-attack that left the French champions chasing shadows. De Bruyne and Phil Foden led the charge, exchanging two one-twos, before the England midfielder delivered a brilliant ball to the back post for Mahrez to tap home. Sensational football.

PSG lost discipline in the closing stages and Angel Di Maria was sent off for a stamp on Fernandinho by the touchline, before Foden rattled the post with a low drive that would have

topped off another world-class display from the City Football Academy graduate.

As well as our free-flowing attacking quality, there were moments of backs-to-the-wall defending, including a fantastic sliding challenge from Zinchenko to deny Neymar inside the area – the new solid and stable version of City in the Champions League in evidence once more.

The celebrations at the full-time whistle said everything. The City players knew the significance of what they had achieved. After losing to Lyon in the quarter-finals the previous season on a desperately disappointing night, this win represented a significant improvement.

This group of players had conquered all before them domestically, but that had not been the case in Europe, where City had lost at the quarter-final stage in each of the previous three campaigns, including the agonising exit to Tottenham Hotspur in 2019.

Before this game against PSG, John Stones called for City to use any negative memories of prior failures as motivation and his rallying cry was certainly heard by his team-mates.

For Guardiola, the result was the culmination of City's hard work over the previous five years. "People believe it's easy to arrive in the final of the Champions League," he said afterwards. "Getting to the final now makes sense of what we have done in the past four or five years."

No one could argue City deserved to go through. We had outclassed PSG, surviving a torrid time in the first half in Paris to win comfortably over two legs. In the 12 Champions League games we had played en route to the final, we had won 11 and drawn one, conceding just four times. City were the first English side to win 11 games in a single European Cup/Champions League campaign – and our run of seven consecutive wins was the longest such run by an English club.

Our unbeaten home run in the competition stretched to a remarkable 14 matches (13 wins and one draw), with the 2-1 loss to Lyon on Matchday 1 in 2018-19 our last defeat at the Etihad.

There was now a steely determination to go with our attacking vitality on the European stage.

"I'm incredibly proud and my first thoughts are with the players who didn't play today," Guardiola said afterwards, showing empathy for his players who had not been involved on such a historic night. "They all deserved to play, everyone has made a contribution and now it is time to enjoy it. We have to win the league and we have two or three weeks to prepare for the final.

"They put a lot of players in the middle, and we struggled a lot in the first half to high press and we changed at half-time. We recovered the ball better in the second half and we were much better in the way we played and 4-1 on aggregate against a team that beat Barcelona and Bayern Munich means a lot to us."

This is what City had wanted for a decade. Our domestic dominance had now translated onto the European scene.

City 5-0 Everton

AGUERO SIGNS OFF IN STYLE ON DAY OF CELEBRATION

23 May 2021

City ended the 2020-21 Premier League campaign in style, beating Everton 5-0 at home, as Sergio Aguero brought the curtain down on his magnificent Etihad career in fitting fashion by scoring two superb goals to take his tally to 260 for the club.

For the first time that season, fans were allowed inside the stadium after Coronavirus restrictions were eased. There may only have been 10,000 of them, but what a difference they made.

City were outstanding and delivered one of the most complete performances of the season. The five-goal margin inflicted on Everton boss Carlo Ancelotti was the heaviest defeat of his illustrious managerial career in what was his 1,167th game in management.

Kevin De Bruyne opened the scoring after 11 minutes, taking a touch to steady Riyad Mahrez's pass before curling brilliantly into the bottom corner, and Gabriel Jesus added a second – his 50th Premier League goal – just three minutes later.

Ruben Dias brought down Richarlison inside the area after the Everton forward had raced clear onto a misplaced pass from Oleksandr Zinchenko. But Ederson saved Gylfi Sigurdsson's penalty and Kyle Walker's brilliant sliding challenge denied Richarlison from the rebound.

Phil Foden scored a brilliant third, finishing smartly after a fine passing move involving Raheem Sterling and Jesus – and then it became the Aguero show. The fans who had chanted his name throughout got their wish to see our all-time leading scorer play one final time at the Etihad, as the 32-year-old replaced Mahrez with 25 minutes remaining.

Aguero was inspired, producing a clever curling shot with the outside of his foot for City's fourth, before a thumping header from Fernandinho's cross made it 5-0. And he nearly managed a hat-trick, being denied only by a smart stop from Jordan Pickford.

It was a fairy-tale finish for the Argentine. This was Aguero's 389th City appearance, and he had now scored a remarkable 260 goals.

Indeed, his double against Everton saw him set yet another significant record, with his 184 Premier League goals the most scored by a player with a single club, eclipsing Wayne Rooney's 183 for Manchester United. Perhaps most impressively, he left English football with the best minutes-to-goals ratio in Premier League history, managing a goal every 109 minutes. Thierry Henry is second on the list with a strike every 122 minutes.

His 260 City goals also mean he is comfortably the club's greatest ever goalscorer, 83 ahead of second-placed Eric Brook, who for 78 years had sat atop the club's scoring chart until Aguero overtook him in November 2017.

It was a dream ending for Aguero on the very pitch that saw him deliver the greatest moment in Premier League history in 2012. Appropriately enough, this was his first double from the bench since his remarkable debut in a 4-0 win against Swansea City in 2011.

"Sergio showed in the last decade his instinct is great, it's fantastic," manager Pep Guardiola declared afterwards.

"He has this gift that his mum and dad gave him, or God, and he will always have it. Sergio helped alongside us to bring this club to the level we have now, he's a special person. It was the perfect end and a fairy-tale moment."

SERGIO AGUERO PREMIER LEAGUE GOALS RECORD

Total Goals	184
Goals (right-footed)	130
Goals (left-footed)	34
Goals (headed)	19
Goals (inside box)	163
Goals (outside box)	21
Goals (penalties)	27
Home	106
Away	78

SERGIO AGUERO MANCHESTER CITY - ALL-TIME GOALS

PLAYER	APP	GOALS
SERGIO AGÜERO	390	260
Eric Brook	493	177
Tommy Johnson	355	166
Joe Hayes	364	153
Colin Bell	501	153

PREMIER LEAGUE ALL TIME GOALS TOTAL

PLAYER	COUNTRY	APP	GOALS
Alan Shearer	England	441	260
Wayne Rooney	England	491	208
Andrew Cole	England	414	187
SERGIO AGUERO	Argentina	275	184
Frank Lampard	England	609	177

PREMIER LEAGUE ALL TIME HAT-TRICKS

PLAYER	COUNTRY	H-T
SERGIO AGUERO	Argentina	12
Alan Shearer	England	11
Robbie Fowler	England	9
Thierry Henry	France	8
Harry Kane	England	8
Michael Owen	England	8

ALL TIME PREMIER LEAGUE MINUTES/GOALS RATIO

PLAYER	APP	GOALS	MINS/GOALS
SERGIO AGUERO	275	184	109
Thierry Henry	258	175	122
Harry Kane	247	166	123
Ruud van Nistelrooy	150	95	128
Mohamed Salah	161	99	131
Luis Suarez	110	69	139
Robin van Persie	280	144	140
Hernan Crespo	49	20	141
Edin Dzeko	130	50	142

It proved one of the most emotional days we had ever experienced at the Etihad. Fans were back in the stadium after 14 long months, the team lifted the Premier League trophy for the third time in four seasons and there was a special farewell ceremony honouring Sergio's enormous contribution to the club over the past decade. The Everton players formed a guard of honour for the City squad ahead of lifting the trophy, and both sets of players then afforded the same tribute to Aguero ahead of his goodbye speech.

Fittingly, the whole post-match ceremony took place in driving Manchester rain.

"My message to the fans is: 'Thank you. Thank you to the City fans for always supporting me," Aguero said during his final interview with the club's media team.

"When you feel the love from your fans, everything is a lot easier. It's the same for anyone in any line of work – when someone believes in you, you do better. I owe a lot to the people at this club because I have the City fans to thank for everything."

There was, however, one more assignment for Aguero and the rest of the City squad in six days' time: our first ever Champions League final.

City 0-1 Chelsea

CITY'S FIRST-EVER CHAMPIONS LEAGUE FINAL APPEARANCE

29 May 2021

City travelled to Portugal on the brink of completing the greatest season in the club's history.

We had already won the Premier League title – our third in four years – and lifted a fourth consecutive Carabao Cup. And now, for the first time ever, we had qualified for the UEFA Champions League final, the biggest game in club football, where we would face Chelsea in Porto.

City's relationship with the Champions League had been difficult. Since qualifying for the competition for the first time back in 2011, we had suffered our fair share of setbacks, including group-stage exits and a couple of chastening experiences in the last 16. Throw in a tortuous VAR disappointment and the overall picture hadn't been good. City had suffered in Europe's premier competition, provoking plenty of criticism in the process.

But this season's version of Manchester City in the Champions League had a different air right from the outset. There was the same intensity and possession-based football, laced with skill and improvised brilliance, augmented by more solidity and pragmatism. The mistakes that had dogged our recent European past had been eradicated, replaced by stoicism and stability.

Our record was hugely impressive. Played 12, won 11, drawn one – just four goals conceded – our only blemish a group-stage draw away at Porto when qualification for the knockout stage had already been secured. We had blitzed our way through and been far and away the best team in the competition going into the showpiece final against a resurgent Chelsea recast since the appointment of Thomas Tuchel as manager four months earlier.

This was our first appearance in a European final for 51 years – the longest gap between European finals in history.

Not since our Cup Winners' Cup triumph in 1970, secured at the Prater Stadion in Vienna after a 2-1 win over Polish side Gornik Zabrze, had City reached a final on the continent.

"I'm the happiest man in the world to be here," manager Pep Guardiola said ahead of the game. "It's a privilege, it's an honour. We're going to try and do our best. All we have to do is be honest with ourselves and try to win the game.

"Sometimes clubs need more finals to win the first one, others need one shot."

Chelsea had been transformed by the appointment of Tuchel, who had taken over from Frank Lampard at the end of January. In the space of 123 days, he had completely altered their fortunes and style, turning what looked to

have been a disastrous season into a memorable one. The German secured a top-four finish, an FA Cup final appearance (where they lost to Leicester) and a place in the Champions League final.

They had also beaten City twice in the lead-up to this match, in the FA Cup semi-final at Wembley and a Premier League game at the Etihad.

Guardiola was looking to become only the fourth manager to win the competition for the fourth time, but Tuchel is no stranger to the competition, either.

After Chelsea knocked out Real Madrid in the semi-final, he became the first man to take two different clubs to the European Cup final in successive seasons, having led Paris Saint-Germain to the previous season's showpiece, where they were beaten 1-0 by Bayern Munich.

It was a match between two heavyweight managers.

Guardiola made a surprise team selection in the final, opting to forgo the use of a defensive-midfielder. Raheem Sterling started, with both Fernandinho and Rodri on the bench. Ilkay Gundogan, our top scorer with 17 in all competitions, was our most defensive-minded midfielder.

It was an attacking line-up but City failed to produce their best football in the final. Chelsea were the better side and created clear chances, winning 1-0 thanks to a first-half strike from Kai Havertz, who collected Mason Mount's ball and rounded Ederson to score.

Indeed, there wasn't a single shot on target from either side after Havertz's 42nd-minute goal. After the way in which we had dismantled

PSG in the semi-final, victories executed with freedom and verve, it was a disappointing performance.

When Kevin De Bruyne departed in the second half, visibly distraught having suffered an acute nose bone and left orbital fractures, it felt then as though this was not to be City's night.

It was Guardiola's first loss in a final as City manager and only the second of his career. It was an unusual feeling, but one which will no doubt make him even more determined to find a winning formula during his remaining years in charge.

Tuchel became just the second manager in history to win three straight games against Guardiola, the latest success adding gloss to a fine four-month period as manager on which he could build.

Sergio Aguero made his final appearance for City, coming off the bench with around 15 minutes remaining as we went in search of an equaliser to take the game into extra time.

But there was to be no repeat of the drama of 93:20.

"It was a tight game and I think, being the first time in the Champions League (final), we played a really good final," Guardiola reflected afterwards. "We showed courage, especially in the second half.

"It's not easy to play this competition for all of us, it's our first time [in the final] but we did everything. I just want to congratulate the players for an exceptional season and the game they played today."

It was a frustrating end to a Champions League campaign that had promised so much for City, but once the pain of the defeat eased, a more measured view of our season could be taken. Two domestic trophies and a clear upturn in form on the European scene meant this had been a fantastic campaign.

Chairman Khaldoon Al Mubarak provided a typically forensic analysis in his annual end-of-season address.

"The domestic league comes first," he said. "That is the foundation for everything. The success in winning the Premier League is what breeds success in every other competition so that is always going to be the foundation.

"We've been very successful in the domestic cup competitions. We have not yet been able to crack the Champions League but we'll crack it. We will crack it. We'll find a way and I have the highest confidence in everyone in our club and our ability to learn and continue to improve."

Losing finals is always painful, particularly when a team plays within itself. But when our Champions League campaign is analysed in full, the improvement is obvious. City now look better equipped than ever to take the final step and win Europe's elite prize.

10 YEARS OF IMPRESSIVE STATS

The numbers that bring home just how successful Manchester City have been over the past decade

Premier League table combining the top seven clubs' performances over the past 10 years:

	Team	P	W	D	L	GF	GA	GD	Pts	PPG
1	MANCHESTER CITY	380	261	58	61	881	335	546	841	2.21
2	Liverpool	380	215	90	75	738	408	330	735	1.93
3	Manchester United	380	215	89	76	676	382	294	734	1.93
4	Chelsea	380	214	84	82	680	397	283	726	1.91
5	Tottenham Hotspur	380	206	81	93	670	419	251	699	1.84
6	Arsenal	380	203	84	93	685	432	253	693	1.82
7	Everton	380	150	107	123	524	476	48	557	1.47

All stats correct up to and including June 1 2021

PREMIER LEAGUE TABLE 2011 • 12

POS	TEAM	P	HOME					AWAY					GD	PTS
			W	D	L	F	A	W	D	L	F	A		
1	MANCHESTER CITY	38	18	1	0	55	12	10	4	5	38	17	+64	89
2	Manchester Utd	38	15	2	2	52	19	13	3	3	37	14	+56	89
3	Arsenal	38	12	4	3	39	17	9	3	7	35	32	+25	70
4	Tottenham Hotspur	38	13	3	3	39	17	7	6	6	27	24	+25	69
5	Newcastle United	38	11	5	3	29	17	8	3	8	27	34	+5	65
6	Chelsea	38	12	3	4	41	24	6	7	6	24	22	+19	64
7	Everton	38	10	3	6	28	15	5	8	6	22	25	+10	56
8	Liverpool	38	6	9	4	24	16	8	1	10	23	24	+7	52
9	Fulham	38	10	5	4	36	26	4	5	10	12	25	-3	52
10	West Bromwich Albion	38	6	3	10	21	22	7	5	7	24	30	-7	47
11	Swansea City	38	8	7	4	27	18	4	4	11	17	33	-7	47
12	Norwich City	38	7	6	6	28	30	5	5	9	24	36	-14	47
13	Sunderland	38	7	7	5	26	17	4	6	9	19	29	-1	45
14	Stoke City	38	7	8	4	25	20	4	4	11	11	33	-17	45
15	Wigan Athletic	38	5	7	7	22	27	6	3	10	20	35	-20	43
16	Aston Villa	38	4	7	8	20	25	3	10	6	17	28	-16	38
17	Queens Park Rangers	38	7	5	7	24	25	3	2	14	19	41	-23	37
18	Bolton	38	4	4	11	23	39	6	2	11	23	38	-31	36
19	Blackburn Rovers	38	6	1	12	26	33	2	6	11	22	45	-30	31
20	Wolverhampton W	38	3	3	13	19	43	2	7	10	21	39	-42	25

PREMIER LEAGUE TABLE 2013 • 14

POS	TEAM	P	HOME					AWAY					GD	PTS
			W	D	L	F	A	W	D	L	F	A		
1	MANCHESTER CITY	38	17	1	1	63	13	10	4	5	39	24	+65	86
2	Liverpool	38	16	1	2	53	18	10	5	4	48	32	+51	84
3	Chelsea	38	15	3	1	43	11	10	4	5	28	16	+44	82
4	Arsenal	38	13	5	1	36	11	11	2	6	32	30	+27	79
5	Everton	38	13	3	3	38	19	8	6	5	23	20	+22	72
6	Tottenham Hotspur	38	11	3	5	30	23	10	3	6	25	28	+4	69
7	Manchester United	38	9	3	7	29	21	10	4	5	35	22	+21	64
8	Southampton	38	8	6	5	32	23	7	5	7	22	23	+8	56
9	Stoke City	38	10	6	3	27	17	3	5	11	18	35	-7	50
10	Newcastle United	38	8	3	8	23	28	7	1	11	20	31	-16	49
11	Crystal Palace	38	8	3	8	18	23	5	3	11	15	25	-15	45
12	Swansea City	38	6	5	8	33	26	5	4	10	21	28	0	42
13	West Ham United	38	7	3	9	25	26	4	4	11	15	25	-11	40
14	Sunderland	38	5	3	11	21	27	5	5	9	20	33	-19	38
15	Aston Villa	38	6	3	10	22	29	4	5	10	17	32	-22	38
16	Hull City	38	7	4	8	20	21	3	3	13	18	32	-15	37
17	West Bromwich Albion	38	4	9	6	24	27	3	6	10	19	32	-16	36
18	Norwich City	38	6	6	7	17	18	2	3	14	11	44	-34	33
19	Fulham	38	5	3	11	24	38	4	2	13	16	47	-45	32
20	Cardiff City	38	5	5	9	20	35	2	4	13	12	39	-42	30

PREMIER LEAGUE TABLE 2017 • 18

POS	TEAM	P	HOME					AWAY					GD	PTS
			W	D	L	F	A	W	D	L	F	A		
1	MANCHESTER CITY	38	16	2	1	61	14	16	2	1	45	13	+79	100
2	Manchester United	38	15	2	2	38	9	10	4	5	30	19	+40	81
3	Tottenham Hotspur	38	13	4	2	40	16	10	4	5	34	20	+38	77
4	Liverpool	38	12	7	0	45	10	9	5	5	39	28	+46	75
5	Chelsea	38	11	4	4	30	16	10	3	6	32	22	+24	70
6	Arsenal	38	15	2	2	54	20	4	4	11	20	31	+23	63
7	Burnley	38	7	5	7	16	17	7	7	5	20	22	-3	54
8	Everton	38	10	4	5	28	22	3	6	10	16	36	-14	49
9	Leicester City	38	7	6	6	25	22	5	5	9	31	38	-4	47
10	Newcastle United	38	8	4	7	21	17	4	4	11	18	30	-8	44
11	Crystal Palace	38	7	5	7	29	24	4	6	9	16	28	-10	44
12	Bournemouth	38	7	5	7	26	30	4	6	9	19	31	-16	44
13	West Ham United	38	7	6	6	24	26	3	6	10	24	42	-20	42
14	Watford	38	7	6	6	27	31	4	2	13	17	33	-20	41
15	Brighton & Hove Albion	38	7	8	4	24	25	2	5	12	10	29	-20	40
16	Huddersfield Town	38	6	5	8	16	25	3	5	11	12	33	-30	37
17	Southampton	38	4	7	8	20	26	3	8	8	17	30	-19	36
18	Swansea City	38	6	3	10	17	24	2	6	11	11	32	-28	33
19	Stoke City	38	5	5	9	20	30	2	7	10	15	38	-33	33
20	West Bromwich Albion	38	3	9	7	21	29	3	4	12	10	27	-25	31

PREMIER LEAGUE TABLE 2018 • 19

POS	TEAM	P	HOME					AWAY					GD	PTS
			W	D	L	F	A	W	D	L	F	A		
1	MANCHESTER CITY	38	18	0	1	57	12	14	2	3	38	11	+72	98
2	Liverpool	38	17	2	0	55	10	13	5	1	34	12	+67	97
3	Chelsea	38	12	6	1	39	12	9	3	7	24	27	+24	72
4	Tottenham Hotspur	38	12	2	5	34	16	11	0	8	33	23	+28	71
5	Arsenal	38	14	3	2	42	16	7	4	8	31	35	+22	70
6	Manchester Utd	38	10	6	3	33	25	9	3	7	32	29	+11	66
7	Wolverhampton W	38	10	4	5	28	21	6	5	8	19	25	+1	57
8	Everton	38	10	4	5	30	21	5	5	9	24	25	+8	54
9	Leicester City	38	7	3	8	24	20	7	4	8	27	28	+3	52
10	West Ham United	38	9	4	6	32	27	3	10	6	20	28	-3	52
11	Watford	38	8	3	8	26	28	6	5	8	26	31	-7	50
12	Crystal Palace	38	5	5	9	19	23	9	2	8	32	30	-2	49
13	Newcastle United	38	8	1	10	24	25	4	8	7	18	23	-6	45
14	Bournemouth	38	8	5	6	30	25	5	1	13	26	45	-14	45
15	Burnley	38	7	2	10	24	32	4	5	10	21	36	-23	40
16	Southampton	38	5	8	6	27	30	4	4	11	18	35	-20	39
17	Brighton & Hove Albion	38	6	5	8	19	28	3	4	12	16	32	-25	36
18	Cardiff City	38	6	2	11	21	38	4	2	13	13	31	-35	34
19	Fulham	38	6	3	10	22	36	1	2	12	12	45	-47	26
20	Huddersfield Town	38	2	3	14	10	31	1	4	14	12	45	-54	16

PREMIER LEAGUE TABLE 2020 • 21

POS	TEAM	P	HOME					AWAY					GD	PTS
			W	D	L	F	A	W	D	L	F	A		
1	MANCHESTER CITY	38	13	2	4	43	17	14	3	2	40	15	+51	86
2	Manchester Utd	38	9	4	6	38	28	12	7	0	35	16	+29	74
3	Liverpool	38	10	3	6	29	20	10	6	3	39	22	+26	69
4	Chelsea	38	9	6	4	31	18	10	4	5	27	18	+22	67
5	Leicester City	38	9	1	9	34	30	11	5	3	34	20	+18	66
6	West Ham United	38	10	4	5	32	22	9	4	6	30	25	+15	65
7	Tottenham Hotspur	38	10	3	6	35	20	8	5	6	33	25	+23	62
8	Arsenal	38	8	4	7	24	21	10	3	6	31	18	+16	61
9	Leeds	38	8	5	6	28	21	10	0	9	34	33	+8	59
10	Everton	38	6	4	9	24	28	11	4	4	23	20	-1	59
11	Aston Villa	38	7	4	8	29	27	9	3	7	26	19	+9	55
12	Newcastle United	38	6	5	8	26	33	6	4	9	20	29	-16	45
13	Wolverhampton W	38	7	4	8	21	25	5	5	9	15	27	-16	45
14	Crystal Palace	38	6	5	8	20	32	6	3	10	21	34	-25	44
15	Southampton	38	8	3	8	28	25	4	4	11	19	43	-21	43
16	Brighton & Hove Albion	38	4	9	6	22	22	5	5	9	18	24	-6	41
17	Burnley	38	4	6	9	14	27	6	3	10	19	28	-22	39
18	Fulham	38	2	4	13	9	28	3	9	7	18	25	-26	28
19	West Bromwich Albion	38	3	6	10	15	39	2	5	12	20	37	-41	26
20	Sheffield United	38	5	1	13	12	27	2	1	16	8	36	-43	23

FA CUP 2010-11

Third Round

9 January 2011, 4pm • Walkers Stadium
Attendance: 31,200 • Referee: Mike Dean

LEICESTER CITY	2	2	MANCHESTER CITY
Bamba 1 King 64			Milner 23 Tevez 45

Third Round Replay

18 January 2011, 7.45pm • Etihad Stadium
Attendance: 27,755 • Referee: Mark Halsey

MANCHESTER CITY	4	2	LEICESTER CITY
Tevez 15 Vieira 37 Johnson 38 Kolarov 90			Gallagher 19 (pen.) Dyer 83

Fourth Round

30 January 2011, 2pm • Meadow Lane
Attendance: 16,587 • Referee: Chris Foy

NOTTS COUNTY	1	1	MANCHESTER CITY
Bishop 59			Dzeko 80

Fourth Round Replay

20 February 2011, 2pm • Etihad Stadium
Attendance: 27,276 • Referee: Mike Jones

MANCHESTER CITY	5	0	NOTTS COUNTY
Vieira 37, 58 Tevez 84 Dzeko 89 Richards 90			

Fifth Round

2 March 2011, 7.45pm • Etihad Stadium
Attendance: 25,570 • Referee: Mark Clattenburg

MANCHESTER CITY	3	0	ASTON VILLA
Y. Touré 5 Balotelli 25 Silva 70			

Quarter-Final

13 March 2011, 4.45pm • Etihad Stadium
Attendance: 41,150 • Referee: Lee Probert

MANCHESTER CITY	1	0	READING
Richards 74			

Semi-Final

16 April 2011, 5.15pm • Wembley Stadium
Attendance: 86,549 • Referee: Mike Dean

MANCHESTER CITY	1	0	MANCHESTER UNITED
Y. Touré 52			Scholes ■72

FINAL

14 May 2011, 3pm • Wembley Stadium
Attendance: 88,643 • Referee: Martin Atkinson

MANCHESTER CITY	1	0	STOKE CITY
Y. Touré 74			

FA CUP 2018-19

Third Round

6 January 2019, 2pm • Etihad Stadium
Attendance: 52,708 • Referee: David Coote

MANCHESTER CITY	7	0	ROTHERHAM UNITED
Sterling 12			
Foden 43			
Ajayi 45+1 (o.g.)			
Gabriel Jesus 52			
Mahrez 73			
Otamendi 78			
Sané 85			

Fourth Round

26 January 2019, 3pm • Etihad Stadium
Attendance: 50,121 • Referee: Graham Scott

MANCHESTER CITY	5	0	BURNLEY
Gabriel Jesus 23			
B. Silva 52			
De Bruyne 61			
Long 73 (o.g.)			
Aguero 85 (pen.)			

Fifth Round

16 February 2019, 5.30pm • Rodney Parade
Attendance: 9,680 • Referee: Andre Marriner

NEWPORT COUNTY	1	4	MANCHESTER CITY
Amond 88			Sané 51
			Foden 75, 89
			Mahrez 90+4

Quarter-Final

16 March 2019, 5.20pm • Liberty Stadium
Attendance: 20,498 • Referee: Andre Marriner

SWANSEA CITY	2	3	MANCHESTER CITY
Grimes 20 (pen.)			B. Silva 69
Celina 29			Nordfeldt 78 (o.g.)
			Aguero 88

Semi-Final

6 April 2019, 5.30pm • Wembley Stadium
Attendance: 71,521 • Referee: Anthony Taylor

MANCHESTER CITY	1	0	BRIGHTON & HOVE ALBION
Gabriel Jesus 4			

FINAL

18 May 2019, 5pm • Wembley Stadium
Attendance: 85,854 • Referee: Kevin Friend

MANCHESTER CITY	6	0	WATFORD
D. Silva 26			
Gabriel Jesus 38, 68			
De Bruyne 61			
Sterling 81, 87			

LEAGUE CUP 2013-14

Third Round

24 September 2013, 7.45pm • Etihad Stadium
Attendance: 25,519 • Referee: Kevin Friend

MANCHESTER CITY	5	0	WIGAN ATHLETIC
Dzeko 33			
Jovetic 60, 83			
Touré 76			
Navas 86			

Fourth Round

30 October 2013, 7.45pm • St James' Park
Attendance: 33,846 • Referee: Neil Swarbrick

NEWCASTLE UNITED	0	2	MANCHESTER CITY
	After Extra Time	Negredo 98	
		Dzeko 105	

Quarter-Final

17 December 2013, 7.45pm • King Power Stadium
Attendance: 31,319 • Referee: Roger East

LEICESTER CITY	1	3	MANCHESTER CITY
Dyer 77			Kolarov 8
			Dzeko 41, 53

Semi-Final, First Leg

8 January 2014, 7.45pm • Etihad Stadium
Attendance: 30,381 • Referee: Jonathan Moss

MANCHESTER CITY	6	0	WEST HAM UNITED
Negredo 12, 26, 49			
Touré 41			
Dzeko 61, 89			

Semi-Final, Second Leg

21 January 2014, 7.45pm • Boleyn Ground, Upton Park
Attendance: 14,390 • Referee: Chris Foy

WEST HAM UNITED	0	3	MANCHESTER CITY
			Negredo 3, 59
			Aguero 24

MANCHESTER CITY WON 9-0 ON AGGREGATE

FINAL

2 March 2014, 2pm • Wembley Stadium
Attendance: 84,697 • Referee: Martin Atkinson

MANCHESTER CITY	3	1	SUNDERLAND
Touré 55			Borini 10
Nasri 56			
Navas 90			

LEAGUE CUP 2015-16

Third Round

22 September 2015, 7.45pm • Stadium of Light
Attendance: 21,644 • Referee: Roger East

SUNDERLAND	1	4	MANCHESTER CITY
Toivonen 83			Aguero 9 (pen.) De Bruyne 25 Mannone 33 (o.g.) Sterling 36

Fourth Round

28 October 2015, 7.45pm • Etihad Stadium
Attendance: 40,585 • Referee: Paul Tierney

MANCHESTER CITY	5	1	CRYSTAL PALACE
Bony 22 De Bruyne 44 Iheanacho 59 Touré 76 (pen.) M. Garcia 90			Delaney 89

Quarter-Final

1 December 2015, 7.45pm • Etihad Stadium
Attendance: 38,246 • Referee: Neil Swarbrick

MANCHESTER CITY	4	1	HULL CITY
Bony 12 Iheanacho 80 De Bruyne 82,87			Robertson 90+2

Semi-Final, First Leg

6 January 2016, 8pm • Goodison Park
Attendance: 34,027 • Referee: Robert Madley

EVERTON	2	1	MANCHESTER CITY
Funes Mori 45 Lukaku 78			Navas 76

Semi-Final, Second Leg

27 January 2016, 7.45pm • Etihad Stadium
Attendance: 50,048 • Referee: Martin Atkinson

MANCHESTER CITY	3	1	EVERTON
Fernandinho 24 De Bruyne 70 Aguero 76			Barkley 18

MANCHESTER CITY WON 4-3 ON AGGREGATE

FINAL

28 February 2016, 4.30pm • Wembley Stadium
Attendance: 86,206 • Referee: Michael Oliver

MANCHESTER CITY	1	1	LIVERPOOL
Fernandinho 49			Coutinho 83
Fernandinho ✘ Navas ✔ Aguero ✔ Touré ✔	After extra time		✔ Can ✘ Lucas ✘ Coutinho ✘ Lallana

MANCHESTER CITY WON 3-1 ON PENALTIES

LEAGUE CUP 2017-18

Third Round

20 September 2017, 8pm • The Hawthorns
Attendance: 14,953 • Referee: Mike Jones

WEST BROMWICH ALBION	1	2	MANCHESTER CITY
Yacob 72			Sané 3, 77

Fourth Round

24 October 2017, 8pm • Etihad Stadium
Attendance: 50,755 • Referee: Kevin Friend

MANCHESTER CITY	0	0	WOLVERHAMPTON WANDERERS
De Bruyne ✔ Touré ✔ Sané ✔ Aguero ✔	After extra time		✔ Bonatini ✘ N'Diaye ✘ Coady

MANCHESTER CITY WON 4-1 ON PENALTIES

Quarter-Final

19 December 2017, 7.45pm • King Power Stadium
Attendance: 31,562 • Referee: Bobby Madley

LEICESTER CITY	1	1	MANCHESTER CITY
Vardy 90+7 (pen.)			B. Silva 26
Fuchs ✔ Maguire ✔ Iborra ✔ Vardy ✘ Mahrez ✘	After extra time		✔ Gundogan ✔ Touré ✔ Nmecha ✔ Gabriel Jesus

MANCHESTER CITY WON 4-3 ON PENALTIES

Semi-Final, First Leg

9 January 2018, 7.45pm • Etihad Stadium
Attendance: 43,426 • Referee: Anthony Taylor

MANCHESTER CITY	2	1	BRISTOL CITY
De Bruyne 55 Aguero 90+2			Reid 44 (pen)

Semi-Final, Second Leg

23 January 2018, 7.45pm • Ashton Gate
Attendance: 26,003 • Referee: Graham Scott

BRISTOL CITY	2	3	MANCHESTER CITY
Pack 64 Flint 90+4			Sané 43 Aguero 49 De Bruyne 90+6

MANCHESTER CITY WON 5-3 ON AGGREGATE

FINAL

25 February 2018, 4.30pm • Wembley Stadium
Attendance: 85,671 • Referee: Craig Pawson

MANCHESTER CITY	3	0	ARSENAL
Aguero 18 Kompany 58 D. Silva 65			

LEAGUE CUP 2018-19

Third Round

25 September 2018, 7.45pm • Kassam Stadium
Attendance: 11,956 • Referee: Roger East

OXFORD UNITED	0	3	MANCHESTER CITY
			Gabriel Jesus 36
			Mahrez 78
			Foden 90+2

Fourth Round

1 November 2018, 7.45pm • Etihad Stadium
Attendance: 35,271 • Referee: Martin Atkinson

MANCHESTER CITY	2	0	FULHAM
Brahim 18, 65			

Quarter-Final

18 December 2018, 7.45pm • King Power Stadium
Attendance: 24,644 • Referee: Lee Mason

LEICESTER CITY	1	1	MANCHESTER CITY
Albrighton 73			De Bruyne 14
Maguire ✔	After		✔ Gundogan
Fuchs ✖	extra		✖ Sterling
Maddison ✖	time		✔ Gabriel Jesus
Soyuncu ✖			✔ Zinchenko

MANCHESTER CITY WON 3-1 ON PENALTIES

Semi-Final, First Leg

9 January 2019, 7.45pm • Etihad Stadium
Attendance: 32,089 • Referee: Mike Dean

MANCHESTER CITY	9	0	BURTON ALBION
De Bruyne 5			
Gabriel Jesus 30, 34, 57, 65			
Zinchenko 37			
Foden 62			
Walker 70			
Mahrez 83			

Semi-Final, Second Leg

23 January 2019, 7.45pm • Pirelli Stadium
Attendance: 6,519 • Referee: Kevin Friend

BURTON ALBION	0	1	MANCHESTER CITY
			Aguero 26

MANCHESTER CITY WON 10-0 ON AGGREGATE

FINAL

24 February 2019, 4.30pm • Wembley Stadium
Attendance: 81,775 • Referee: Jonathan Moss

CHELSEA	0	0	MANCHESTER CITY
Jorginho ✖			✔ Gundogan
Azpilicueta ✔	After		✔ Aguero
Emerson ✔	extra		✖ Sané
Luiz ✖	time		✔ B. Silva
Hazard ✔			✔ Sterling

MANCHESTER CITY WON 4-3 ON PENALTIES

LEAGUE CUP 2019-20

Third Round

24 September 2019, 7.45pm • Deepdale
Attendance: 22,025 • Referee: Lee Mason

PRESTON NORTH END	0	3	MANCHESTER CITY
			Sterling 19
			Gabriel Jesus 35
			Ledson 42 (o.g.)

Fourth Round

29 October 2019, 7.45pm • Etihad Stadium
Attendance: 37,143 • Referee: Jonathan Moss

MANCHESTER CITY	3	1	SOUTHAMPTON
Otamendi 20			Stephens 75
Aguero 38, 56			

Quarter-Final

18 December 2019, 7.45pm • Kassam Stadium
Attendance: 11,817 • Referee: Andrew Madley

OXFORD UNITED	1	3	MANCHESTER CITY
Taylor 46			Cancelo 22
			Sterling 50, 70

Semi-Final, First Leg

7 January 2020, 8pm • Old Trafford
Attendance: 69,023 • Referee: Mike Dean

MANCHESTER UNITED	1	3	MANCHESTER CITY
Rashford 70			B. Silva 17
			Mahrez 33
			Pereira 38 (o.g.)

Semi-Final, Second Leg

29 January 2020, 7.45pm • Etihad Stadium
Attendance: 51,000 • Referee: Kevin Friend

MANCHESTER CITY	0	1	MANCHESTER UNITED
			Matic 35

MANCHESTER CITY WON 3-2 ON AGGREGATE

FINAL

1 March 2020, 4.30pm • Wembley Stadium
Attendance: 82,145 • Referee: Lee Mason

ASTON VILLA	1	2	MANCHESTER CITY
Samatta 41			Aguero 20
			Rodri 30

LEAGUE CUP 2020-21

Third Round

24 September 2020, 7.45pm • Etihad Stadium
Attendance: 0 • Referee: Jonathan Moss

MANCHESTER CITY	2	1	BOURNEMOUTH
Delap 18 Foden 75			Surridge 22

Fourth Round

30 September 2020, 7pm • Turf Moor
Attendance: 0 • Referee: Andrew Madley

BURNLEY	0	3	MANCHESTER CITY
			Sterling 35, 49 Torres 65

Quarter-Final

22 December 2020, 8pm • Emirates Stadium
Attendance: 0 • Referee: Stuart Attwell

ARSENAL	1	4	MANCHESTER CITY
Lacazette 31			Gabriel Jesus 3 Mahrez 54 Foden 59 Laporte 73

Semi-Final

6 January 2021, 8pm • Old Trafford
Attendance: 34,027 • Referee: Martin Atkinson

MANCHESTER UNITED	0	2	MANCHESTER CITY
			Stones 50 Fernandinho 83

FINAL

25 April 2021, 4.30pm • Wembley Stadium
Attendance: 7,773 • Referee: Paul Tierney

MANCHESTER CITY	1	0	TOTTENHAM HOTSPUR
Laporte 82			

COMMUNITY SHIELD 2012

12 August 2012, 1.30pm • Villa Park
Attendance: 36,394 • Referee: Kevin Friend

CHELSEA	2	3	MANCHESTER CITY
Torres 40 Bertrand 80			Y. Touré 53 Tevez 59 Nasri 65

COMMUNITY SHIELD 2018

5 August 2018, 3pm • Wembley Stadium
Attendance: 72,724 • Referee: Jonathan Moss

CHELSEA	0	2	MANCHESTER CITY
			Aguero 13, 58

COMMUNITY SHIELD 2019

4 August 2019, 3pm • Wembley Stadium
Attendance: 77,565 • Referee: Martin Atkinson

LIVERPOOL	1	1	MANCHESTER CITY
Matip 77			Sterling 12
Shaqiri ✔ Wijnaldum ✖ Lallana ✔ Oxlade-Chamberlain ✔ Salah ✔	After extra time		✔ Gundogan ✔ B. Silva ✔ Foden ✔ Zinchenko ✔ Gabriel Jesus

MANCHESTER CITY WON 5-4 ON PENALTIES

The top 10 goalscorers in the Premier League over the decade

Player	Goals	Games Played	Mins/ Goal
Aguero, Sergio	184	275	107.92
Kane, Harry	166	245	122.3
Vardy, Jamie	118	245	169.94
Lukaku, Romelu	113	252	168.83
Mohamed Salah	97	158	130.62
Sterling, Raheem	96	290	229.65
Mane, Sadio	95	229	187.72
Rooney, Wayne	91	207	180.36
Giroud, Olivier	90	255	160.58
Hazard, Eden	85	245	228.85

All stats correct up to and including June 1 2021

The only two clubs to win each of the Premier League, FA Cup, League Cup and Community Shield over this period are Manchester City and Manchester United.

CITY
Premier League x5,
FA Cup x2,
League Cup x6,
Community Shield x3

UNITED
Premier League x1,
FA Cup x1,
League Cup x1,
Community Shield x4

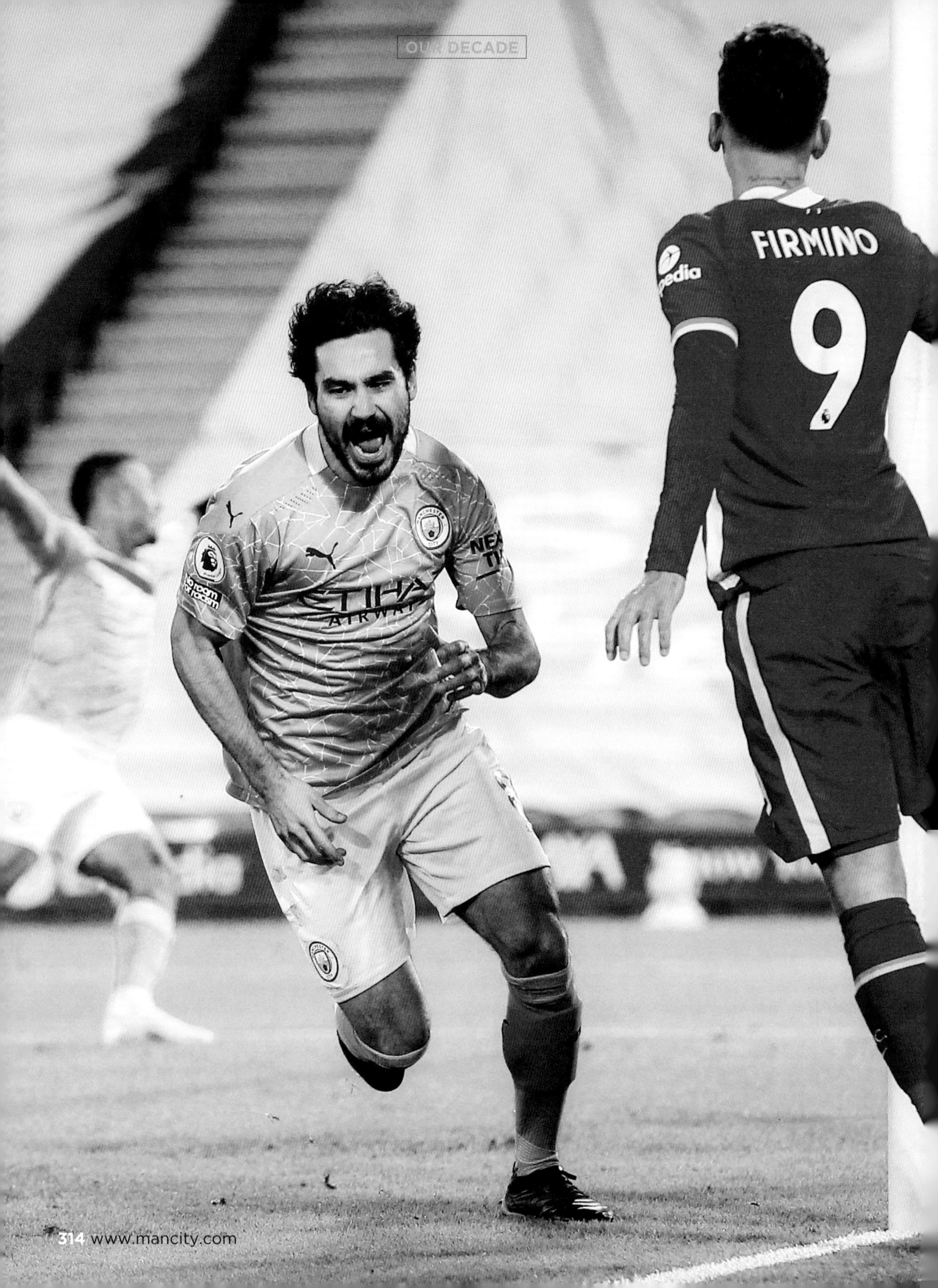
FIRMINO
9
ETIHAD AIRWAYS
No room for racism

TABLE TOPPERS

TEAM	GAMES WON
MANCHESTER CITY	**261**
Liverpool	215
Manchester United	215
Chelsea	214
Tottenham Hotspur	206

TEAM	GOALS
MANCHESTER CITY	**881**
Liverpool	738
Arsenal	685
Chelsea	680
Manchester United	676

TEAM	SHOT CONVERSION RATE (%)
MANCHESTER CITY	**13.19**
Arsenal	12.62
Manchester United	12.58
Leicester City	11.97
Leeds United	11.88

TEAM	POSSESSION
MANCHESTER CITY	**62.74**
Liverpool	59.25
Leeds United	57.77
Arsenal	57.61
Chelsea	57.39

TEAM	CLEAN SHEETS
MANCHESTER CITY	**167**
Manchester United	144
Chelsea	143
Liverpool	140
Arsenal	131

All stats correct up to and including June 1 2021